PATIOS AND GARDEN WALLS

TIME
LIFE
BOOKS

This volume is part of a series offering home owners detailed instructions on repairs, construction and improvements which they can undertake themselves.

HOME REPAIR
AND IMPROVEMENT

PATIOS AND GARDEN WALLS

BY THE EDITORS OF
TIME-LIFE BOOKS

TIME-LIFE BOOKS
AMSTERDAM

TIME-LIFE BOOKS

EUROPEAN EDITOR: Kit van Tulleken
Assistant European Editor: Gillian Moore
Design Director: Ed Skyner
Chief of Research: Vanessa Kramer
Chief Sub-Editor: Ilse Gray

HOME REPAIR AND IMPROVEMENT

EDITORIAL STAFF FOR PATIOS AND GARDEN WALLS
Series Director: Jackie Matthews
Text Director: Charles Boyle
Editors: Chris Farman, Martin Leighton
Writer/Researcher: Fergus Fleming
Researcher: Caroline Manyon
Designer: Paul Reeves
Design Assistants: Andy Monks, Mike Snell
Sub-Editors: Jane Hawker, Hilary Hockman

EDITORIAL PRODUCTION
Co-ordinator: Nikki Allen
Assistant: Maureen Kelly
Editorial Department: Theresa John, Debra Lelliott

THE CONSULTANTS: Paul Davis, a member of the Guild of Bricklayers, has
been teaching at the Hammersmith and West London College since 1979.

Leslie Stokes was a self-employed carpenter and joiner for seven years,
specializing in purpose-made joinery and internal fittings. Since 1976 he
has taught in the building department at the Hammersmith and West
London College.

Contents

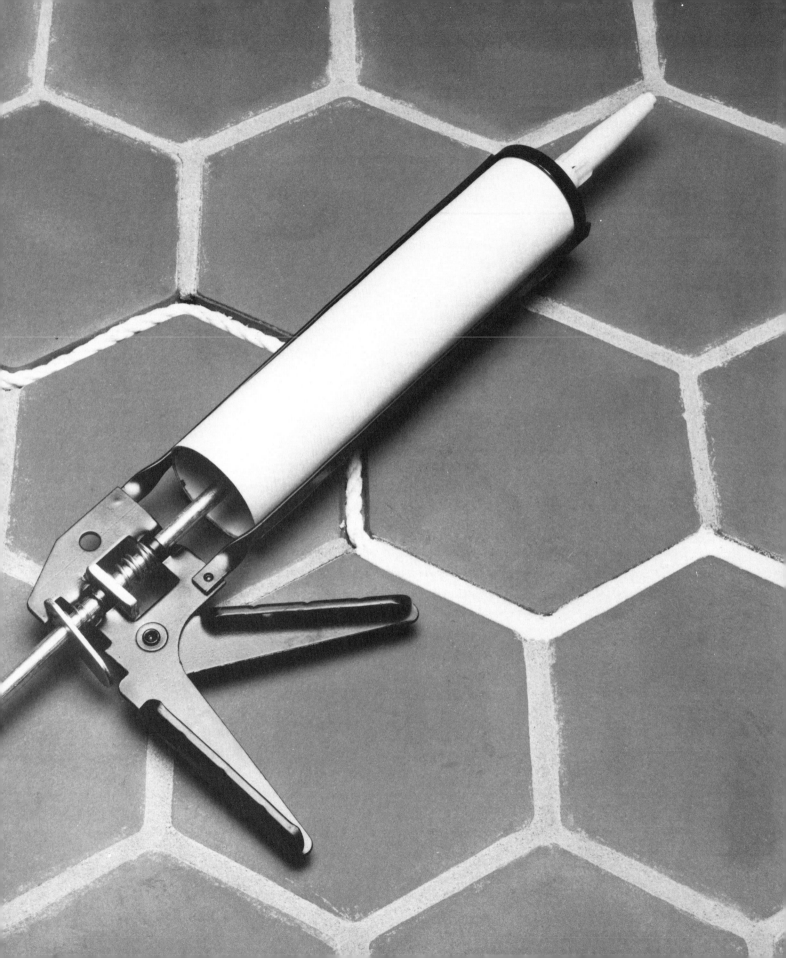

Making the Outdoors Habitable

Flexible jointing. A caulking gun charged with flexible sealant rests on the hexagonal ceramic tiles of a patio. To prevent fractures in the paving joints caused by settlement of the underlying concrete slab, the gaps running between the tiles that lie over an expansion joint are packed with caulking rope, then finished with a silicone or polysulphide sealant; all other joints between tiles are filled with mortar grout.

In the right season, the urge to relax in the open air and enjoy the benefits of sun and nature are as strong as people's need to seek shelter in less hospitable climatic periods. From earliest architectural history, the patio has provided an important transitional point between the shelter of the house and mankind's emulation of nature—the garden.

A patio is essentially a masonry platform set at ground level that provides an outdoor living area. It may be formal or informal, depending on its shape and the materials used to build it. Bricks or paving stones set in sand or concrete are very much more casual than an elegantly veneered surface of ceramic tiles. Walls, archways, steps and paved paths constructed with similar materials to those used to veneer a patio will integrate the patio with the surrounding garden; alternatively, the garden can be integrated more closely with the house itself by enclosing the patio in timber and glass to create a conservatory in which exotic or delicate plant species can be grown.

When deciding where to site a patio, such factors as the orientation of the house and the direction of the prevailing winds must be taken into account. You may have to choose between capturing the maximum of the morning or afternoon sun, or it may be necessary to provide shade from the heat of the midday sun. On an exposed coast or hillside, the prevailing winds could spoil sunbathing; on the other hand, cooling breezes on days of torrid heat could be welcome.

You may also want to consider the presence of a favourite shade tree whose roots, stretching out as far as the tips of the branches, should be disturbed as little as possible. A heavy layer of soil topped by a concrete slab will smother that root system, depriving it of air and water. On the other hand, the tree roots, pushing up to the surface in search of air and water, could destroy the paving.

If you want a tree and a patio to coexist peacefully, choose a paving material that can be laid in sand, so that water can trickle down between the bricks or stones. In addition, leave half a metre or so of open space around the trunk of the tree, and regularly give the tree an extra ration of water—preferably through permanent holes driven into the ground towards the roots—so that the roots will be encouraged to stay well below the patio surface.

Cost is another important factor to consider. Tiles are the most expensive surfacing material—costing, with their concrete base, more than twice as much as a plain concrete slab, and three times as much as bricks set in sand. Although flagstones are also usually expensive, you will probably be able to buy them cheaper if you happen to live near a stone or slate quarry. Using an indigenous material has another advantage: it should result in a patio whose colours and textures blend more harmoniously into the landscape.

Planning and Preparing for a Concrete Slab

A concrete slab, free-form or rectangular, is the solid base of many garden patios. The concrete can be given a variety of decorative finishes (pages 19–21) and can also be paved with bricks or tiles.

Pouring a slab requires careful preparation. It is advisable to check your plans with the local authorities, for although permission may not be needed for laying a patio, it will probably be required for a structure erected over it. Your planning will also be influenced by the stability of the earth over which the slab is to be laid. If there have been recent deep landfills, or if water is found within 300 mm of the ground surface, seek professional advice.

In deciding the location and size of the slab, consider first whether you want a sunny or shaded patio. Ensure that the patio will be in proportion to the house by experimenting with a hose-pipe laid out in different geometric forms on the site. You will also have to consider any obstacles to the excavation such as trees, septic tanks or sewer inspection chambers. Make a scale drawing that shows existing structures and landscape features.

Site preparation begins with laying out the perimeter of the slab with stakes and string. To ensure that the sides of a rectangular slab are square to the house, use the 3–4–5 method of triangulation in which two steel tape measures are extended from the house wall to form a right-angled triangle (opposite page, below).

Once the site has been dug out and levelled, the form boards are installed in such a way that, after the concrete is poured, the slab will slope away from the house to allow water to drain. Generally, slabs should be 100 to 150 mm thick, depending on the local climate, and should slope 10 to 15 mm in every metre. The forms are constructed from 18 mm plywood, professionally known as shuttering ply, which is water resistant and relatively inexpensive; alternatively, you can use lengths of old timber such as floorboards. Because wet concrete exerts considerable outward pressure, the shuttering is supported by stakes and 50 by 50 mm runners along the top edge of the board.

In most situations, an unreinforced concrete slab 100 mm thick can be poured in one piece provided that its area does not exceed 12 square metres. Slabs larger in area should be divided into smaller units separated by expansion joints, which allow each unit to shift independently of the others with earth movement and so avoid stresses that may cause the slab to crack. Expansion joints consist of strips of asphalt-impregnated filler and, in addition to dividing the concrete sections, they separate slabs from contiguous rigid structures such as the house wall itself as well as downpipes or water drains.

The slab is laid on a layer of hardcore with a sand blinding which acts as a drainage bed and keeps the slab dry. For a 100 mm-thick slab in an average climate and on sandy soil, the drainage bed should be 50 to 100 mm deep; in clay or rocky soil, a 150 mm drainage bed may be needed. A wire-mesh grid supported 50 mm above the drainage bed may be essential in areas prone to earth movement, holding the slab together if small cracks develop.

When the excavation is prepared, calculate the amount of hardcore and concrete you need by using the chart below. For a free-form slab, use the method shown opposite, above, to estimate the area to be covered, then refer to the chart. Mix the concrete in a hired mixer, or have it delivered, ready mixed, by a contractor.

Both hardcore and concrete can be rough on clothes and hands, so wear kneepads and gloves. When breaking up hardcore with a club hammer, wear goggles.

Estimating Materials for Concrete Slabs

Estimating cubic quantities. To determine the amount of hardcore and concrete required for a drainage bed and slab, calculate the area to be covered, in square metres. Locate the closest figure in the left-hand column of the chart on the right, and read across that row to the column corresponding with the proposed thickness of the hardcore or slab, in millimetres. Then add 8 per cent to the volume indicated, to compensate for waste and spillage.

Area of slab	Thickness of hardcore or slab				
	50 mm	75 mm	100 mm	125 mm	150 mm
1 sq. m.	0.05 cu. m.	0.075 cu. m.	0.1 cu. m.	0.125 cu.m	0.15 cu. m.
2.5 sq. m.	0.125 cu. m.	0.188 cu. m.	0.25 cu. m.	0.313 cu. m.	0.375 cu. m.
5 sq. m.	0.25 cu. m.	0.375 cu. m.	0.5 cu. m.	0.625 cu. m.	0.75 cu. m.
10 sq. m.	0.5 cu. m.	0.75 cu. m.	1 cu. m.	1.25 cu. m.	1.5 cu. m.
20 sq. m.	1 cu. m.	1.5 cu. m.	2 cu. m.	2.5 cu. m.	3 cu. m.
30 sq. m.	1.5 cu. m.	2.25 cu. m.	3 cu. m.	3.75 cu. m.	4.5 cu. m.
40 sq. m.	2 cu. m.	3 cu. m.	4 cu. m.	5 cu. m.	6 cu. m.
50 sq. m.	2.5 cu. m.	3.75 cu. m.	5 cu. m.	6.25 cu. m.	7.5 cu. m.

Finding the area of a free-form slab. Decide the approximate size and shape of the free-form slab by laying a hose-pipe in the garden and then transfer this shape on to graph paper with the sides of the squares representing 500 mm. Assign a rough fractional value to each square partially covered by the slab. Then add up the full squares and the fractions to find the approximate area of the proposed slab. Use this figure and the chart on the opposite page to calculate the quantity of hardcore and concrete you will need.

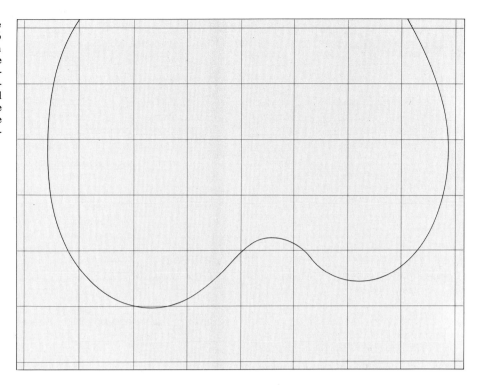

Excavating and Grading a Rectangular Slab

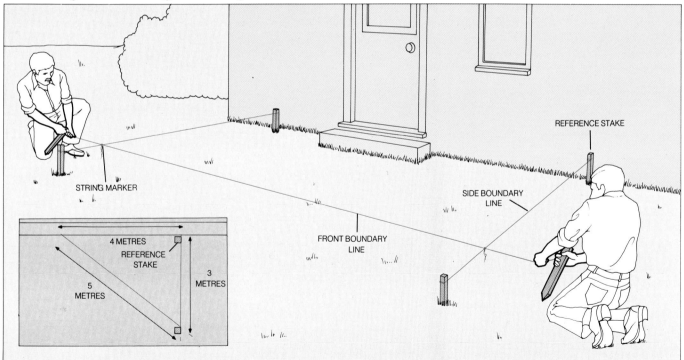

REFERENCE STAKE

STRING MARKER

SIDE BOUNDARY
LINE

FRONT BOUNDARY
LINE

4 METRES

REFERENCE
STAKE

5
METRES

3
METRES

1 Laying out the site. Drive in two reference stakes at the planned edge of the slab against the house wall, and at each reference stake use the 3–4–5 method of triangulation to establish a right angle for the side boundary lines *(inset)*. Stretch steel tapes from a reference stake and from a point 4 metres along the wall, and drive a steel peg into the ground at the point where the 3 metre mark

of the tape attached to the stake intersects the 5 metre mark of the second tape. Repeat the process for the other stake.

Lay out the side boundary lines with strings attached to two stakes driven into the ground 600 mm beyond the planned length of the sides. Then measure back 600 mm from the stakes, and tie string markers to the boundary strings.

Cut a third piece of string which is 1200 mm longer than the distance between the strings marking the side boundaries. Then, with the aid of a helper, stretch this string across the side boundary strings and at right angles to them, lining it up with the string markers and anchoring it to stakes driven in 600 mm beyond the point where the strings intersect.

2 **Digging out the site.** Dig a trench 250 mm deep and 350 mm wide outside the front and side boundary lines. Then, working in parallel rows back and forth between the perimeter trenches, dig out the area enclosed by the trench. Save turf to fill in at the sides of the finished slab.

Level the ground with a shovel, making certain there is no loose soil from previous infills. Pack any hollows with hardcore broken down into small pieces with a club hammer. Use a long timber straightedge to check the ground is level, then dampen the area with a hose. Compact the surface with a tamper—a 600 mm square of 18 mm plywood with a braced handle 1200 mm high made of 100 by 50 mm timber.

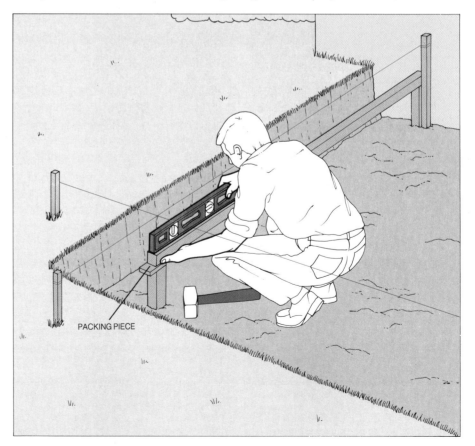

PACKING PIECE

3 **Establishing the grade.** Drive a 50 by 50 mm stake into the ground immediately outside one of the reference stakes at the house wall; the height of the stake should be the planned height of the slab less 50 mm. Drive in another 50 by 50 mm stake on the inside of the front boundary string and on the outside of the side boundary string.

Place a long, rigid straightedge on top of the two stakes. Calculate the fall for water runoff required *(page 8)* and cut a timber packing piece to the difference in height between the back and front of the slab. Insert the packing piece between the stake farthest from the house and the straightedge resting on it. With a club hammer, knock the stake into the ground until the straightedge is level. Repeat this process for the other side of the slab, after first checking that the two stakes against the house wall are level. To ensure the stability of the form, install intermediate stakes at intervals of about 1 metre.

4 **Installing the side form boards.** Rip a piece of 18 mm shuttering ply about 200 mm longer than the side of the planned slab and the same width as the slab height. Cut a runner of 50 by 50 mm timber to the same length as the shuttering ply and nail the runner flush to one edge of the board *(right)*. Place the runner over the top of the side stakes, with the ply inwards and butted firmly against the house wall, and nail the ply to the stakes from the inside of the form. Install the opposite side board in the same way.

5 **Completing the form.** Using the front boundary string as a guide, drive in two stakes to support the ends of the front form board. Nail the side form boards to the new stakes. Drive in intermediate stakes along the front boundary string at 1 metre intervals, then remove the strings. Cut a length of shuttering ply to the exact distance between the two side form boards and to the same width as the side board, and attach a runner *(Step 4, above)*. Nail the front form board to the stakes *(inset)*.

If two lengths of shuttering must be butted together, install additional stakes 200 mm on either side of the joint. Reinforce the joint with an additional piece of plywood nailed to the back of the boards under the runner.

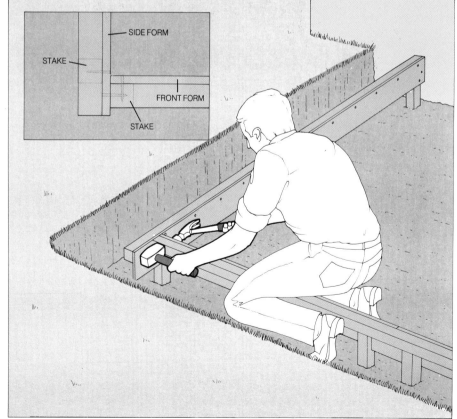

SIDE FORM

STAKE

FRONT FORM

STAKE

6 **Installing joint filler.** Lay a continuous strip of expansion joint filler cut to the intended thickness of the slab against the wall of the house and any steps, supporting it at intervals with handfuls of hardcore. Install the divider forms in the same way as the side forms *(page 11)*, ensuring that the stakes are on the outside of the first area to be concreted. Lay a strip of joint filler against the inside of the divider.

JOINT FILLER

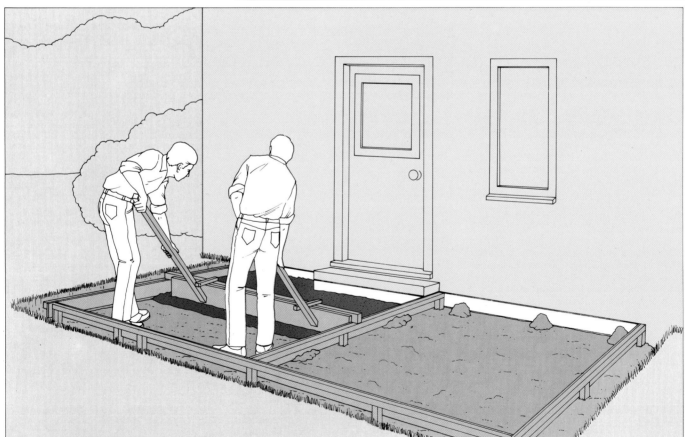

7 **Laying and levelling the hardcore base.** Wearing kneepads, gloves and goggles, use a club hammer to break up and level hardcore in the area to be concreted. The depth of the drainage bed will vary according to the conditions described on page 8. Cover the hardcore with a 25 mm blinding of builders' sand. With a helper, level the sand by dragging a screed rail over it, making sure that no lumps of hardcore protrude above the surface and that there are no hollows.

To make the screed rail, cut a 200 by 25 mm board 50 mm shorter than the distance between the forms, and a 100 by 50 mm piece of timber 250 mm longer than this distance. Nail them together with the wider board centred over the narrower one. To the face of the narrow board attach two 50 by 50 mm handles, each 1.2 metres long and cut at an angle of 30 degrees at the bottom. Brace the handles with 50 by 50 mm timbers nailed across the top of the screed rail.

8 **Laying wire mesh.** Wearing gloves, lay sheets of 6 mm 200 by 200 mm wire mesh over the blinding; leave a 50 mm gap between the edge of the mesh and the perimeter of the area being concreted. Overlap adjacent sheets by one square and bind them together with short lengths of wire. With bolt croppers, trim the mesh to fit around steps, divider forms and other obstacles. Before pouring the concrete, the mesh must be lifted about 50 mm above the drainage bed by concrete or plastic spacers placed under the mesh at 1 metre intervals.

Installing Permanent Form Boards

1 **Plotting the pattern.** To divide a rectangular slab into smaller rectangular units of varied sizes, each framed permanently with wooden strips, outline the slab on graph paper, with the sides of the squares representing 500 mm. Divide the scale drawing into four equal quadrants, the primary forms; then subdivide one quadrant into the desired pattern of squares and rectangles. Repeat this pattern in the other three quadrants.

Extend all the pattern lines to the perimeter of the drawing, creating a grid that will serve as a guide for the placement of strings along the form boards of the actual slab. These strings will indicate where extra form boards are needed within each quadrant for shaping the secondary forms. Plot the stake locations for these forms on the scale drawing, marking each with an X.

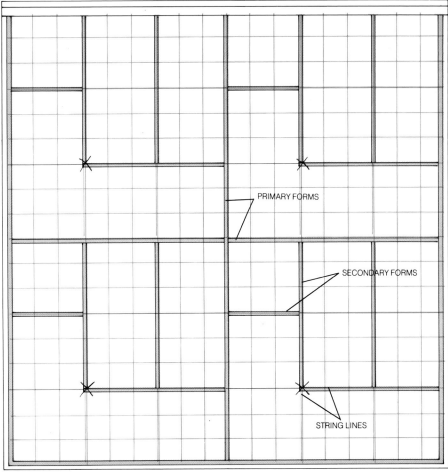

PRIMARY FORMS

SECONDARY FORMS

STRING LINES

2 **Setting up the primary forms.** Cut the primary form boards from 100 by 50 mm pressure-treated timber for additional resistance to weather. To install the form boards, use the techniques shown on pages 10–11; however, in this case, set the stakes 25 mm lower than the top of the boards so they will be hidden under the concrete, omit the runners, and nail the boards to the outside of the stakes with galvanized nails.

Add joint filler to the house wall and any steps and lay a hardcore bed with sand blinding *(page 12)*, then install a string grid for the secondary forms with the strings stretching from the bottoms of the boards. Tie strings against the house wall to pegs driven in next to the joint filler. Measure to make sure the strings are even with the slightly sloping bottom edges of the side form boards. Drive in 100 by 50 mm support stakes at the marked locations; remove hardcore as necessary and sink the stakes into the ground until the strings just touch their tops. With all stakes in place, mark the location of the grid strings on the primary forms; then remove the strings.

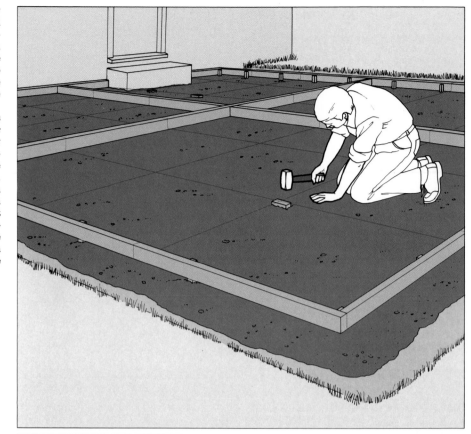

3 **Installing the secondary forms.** Cut 100 by 50 mm form boards to fit the dimensions of the pattern. Rest one end of a form board on its stake, covering half the stake, and toenail a 75 mm nail through the board into the top of the stake. Complete the corner by resting the adjoining board on the other half of the stake, toenailing it to the stake. Then nail the second board to the end of the first.

Where a secondary form board butts into the face of any other form board, drive two nails through that board into the end of the secondary board. Because the slab is divided into small sections, mesh is not necessary, but drive 75 mm nails part way into the inside faces of the primary form boards and into both faces of the secondary form boards, leaving about 40 mm of the nail exposed; the protruding ends will anchor the concrete. In driving in the nails, cushion the blows by holding a club hammer against the opposite face, to keep the forms from shifting. Finally, before pouring the concrete, cover the top edges of the form boards with heavy-duty masking tape.

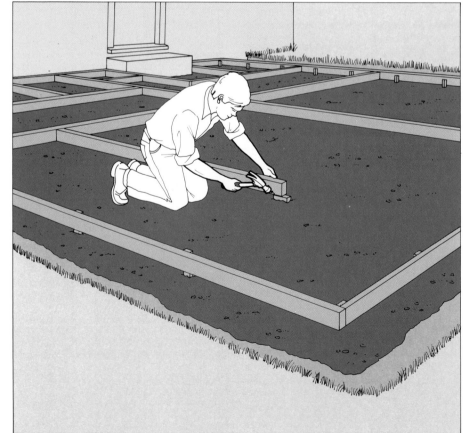

Building a Curved Form for a Free-Form Slab

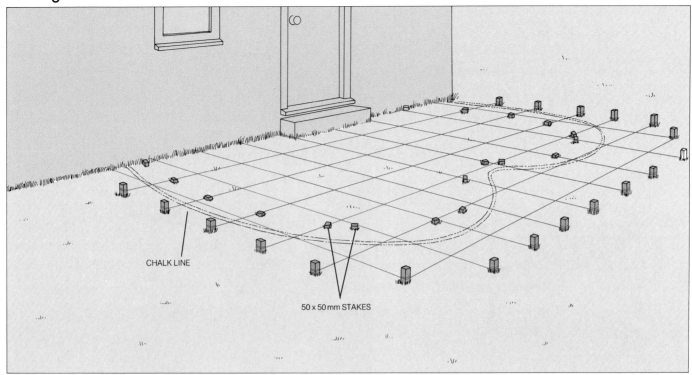

CHALK LINE

50 x 50 mm STAKES

1 Marking out and excavating the site. Over the slab site, install a grid with strings and pegs set at 500 mm intervals. Adjust the strings to the planned height of the slab top, allowing for a drainage slope as described on page 8. Taking measurements from your scale plan of the slab *(page 9)*, drive in 50 by 50 mm stakes at least 450 mm long at the points where the slab outline crosses the grid strings. Along particularly tight curves, use the scale plan, a measuring tape and a builder's square to plot positions for intermediate stakes between any pair of stakes more than 300 mm apart. Drive the stakes into the ground to the same height as the graded strings of the grid.

Mark a chalk line 300 mm outside the perimeter of the slab outline *(above)*. Remove the strings and excavate the area enclosed by the chalk line to a depth which is equal to the thicknesses of the drainage bed and the slab added together. Remove all loose soil and level the floor of the excavation as shown on page 10, using the stakes as a guide to the gradient necessary for water runoff.

2 Installing form boards. Butt the end of a 2400 mm length of 6 mm lath against the house wall and tack it to the inside of the stakes. Mark the lath 100 mm beyond the last stake it crosses. Cut a form board from 12 mm shuttering ply to the length marked on the lath and to the width required. Working inside the stakes, nail the form board flush with the tops of the stakes with 25 mm galvanized nails. Butt the lath against the end of the installed form board, and use the procedure described above to measure, cut and install the next form board; continue in this way until the form is completed.

Where two form boards are butted together, nail a 200 mm-long panel of reinforcing plywood over the join with one side against the nearby stake. Drive in a new stake against the form board on the other side of the panel and nail the form to the stake *(inset)*. In tight curves, where a form board cannot be bent against the stakes, notch the back of the board with saw cuts 12 to 20 mm apart to make it more pliable. Lay joint filler against the house and, if expansion joints are necessary, add straight form boards, also lined with joint filler.

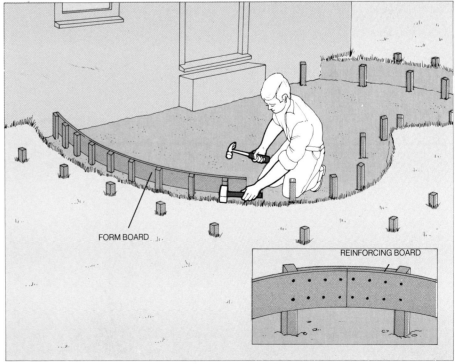

FORM BOARD

REINFORCING BOARD

3 **Checking the grading grid.** Replace a sufficient number of the grid strings to check that the curved form is still at the proper height and grade. If necessary, lift or hammer down the boards and stakes. Check that the floor of the excavation matches the slope of the grade. The strings and pegs can now be removed. Lay down the joint filler, hardcore and a sand blinding *(page 12, Step 7)*.

4 **Cutting mesh to fit the form.** Lay a sheet of wire mesh over a section of the form, allowing it to overlap the curve of the form boards where necessary. Cut the mesh along the curve, 50 mm in from the form, using bolt croppers, and remove the trimmed mesh. Cut additional sections of mesh, allowing each to overlap the previous section by one square, and tie them together with short lengths of wire. Before pouring the concrete, place spacers every metre under the mesh.

Pouring and Finishing the Paved Surface

The key requirement for pouring and finishing a concrete slab is speed. On a dry, windy day, it may take as little as three hours for freshly poured concrete to become too stiff to work. To be sure of getting the job done in time, enlist the aid of helpers. For a 4 by 3 metre slab, three or four people will need about an hour for the heavy work of pouring, levelling and smoothing the concrete, plus another two to three hours to finish the surface. Unless you are quite sure about completing a slab of the size you have planned in one day, it will be best to carry out the work in stages, leaving a week between pouring and finishing each section.

Calculate in advance the amount of concrete required using the chart on page 8. Dry-packed mixes are available in packages up to 50 kilograms and are economical for small jobs as there is little wastage. If you are mixing concrete yourself or ordering it, the proportions (in volume) for exposed pavings are 1 part cement to 2 parts sand and 3 of 20 mm aggregate. For slabs that are to be given a brick or tile veneer, the ratio is 1:2½:3½.

If you wish to colour the concrete, special pigments can be added at the mixing stage; however, the pigment and concrete ingredients must be mixed in very precise measurements to ensure proper colour conformity between batches. For a pebble-aggregate surface *(pages 20–21)*, use pea gravel, 10 mm aggregate or crushed rock aggregate; order 20 kilograms for every square metre. Cross-sections of hardwood for embedding in concrete *(page 21)* are available in rounds from tree surgeons or nurseries, and must be carefully treated with preservative to inhibit rot.

For slabs requiring over 5 cubic metres of concrete, you can save time and work by having it delivered ready mixed in a lorry. Get the lorry to park on the street, then lay a path of planks up to the site of the slab and transport the concrete over the planks in wheelbarrows. For smaller quantities, some contractors offer an on-the-spot mixing service using a concrete mixer mounted on the back of a light truck. Alternatively, you can hire an electric or petrol-driven mixer and mix the concrete yourself—the concrete should be just wet enough to stick to a shovel, and not so dry that it forms a clump.

Before pouring the concrete, grease or hose down the forms to prevent the wet concrete from sticking to them. Carry the concrete to the forms in loads of half a wheelbarrow, running the barrows over planks laid up to the form boards.

For levelling and smoothing the concrete, specialist tools include a skip float *(page 18, below)* and—for shaping the edges of the slab—an edging tool, sometimes known as an arrissing tool, shown on page 19. You can make your own skip float by first bevelling and sanding a 25 mm board 1 metre long and 200 mm wide. Then attach the pivoting handle with a bolt passed through two blocks of wood screwed to the centre of the float.

Compacting the concrete causes moisture, known as "bleed water", to rise to the surface. Before finishing the concrete or applying a decorative surface texture, wait until the bleed water has completely evaporated—this takes anything from 20 minutes to two hours.

After the slab is finished, it must be "cured"—kept moist and warm for at least a week—to allow it to reach its full structural strength. Usually the slab is covered with a polythene sheet, but coloured slabs and pebble-aggregate surfaces are air-cured—left uncovered and sprinkled several times a day with water. The forms are only removed after the slab is cured.

Direct skin contact with wet concrete should be avoided, so wear gloves. It is also advisable to wear Wellington boots to protect your clothing.

Filling the Forms

1 Adding the concrete: Dump enough concrete into the first form to fill a metre-wide section across the bed between the form boards. Use a shovel to push the concrete into the corners of the form and to pack each successive load against the preceding one. Overfill the form by about 12 mm.

After filling the section, drive a shovel between the inner edges of the form and the concrete to force the coarse aggregate away from the sides. Then jab the spade vertically into the concrete throughout the section to eliminate air pockets. If the wire reinforcement sags into the drainage bed under the weight of the concrete, pull it up with a wire hook so that it is embedded in the middle of the concrete.

2 **Tamping the concrete.** As each section is filled, set a tamping beam—a straight 100 by 50 mm piece of timber or metal cut 600 mm wider than the width of the form—on edge across the form boards. With the aid of a helper, lift and lower the tamping beam in a chopping motion to force the aggregate down into the concrete. Then pull the tamping beam across the surface of the concrete, simultaneously sliding it from side to side in a saw-like motion. Tilt the tamping beam towards you as you pull it, so that the bottom of the board acts as a cutting edge. Repeat this action to level any remaining low spots or bumps.

Fill and level the rest of the form in sections, then move to the next form. When you cannot operate the tamping beam from outside a form because adjacent forms are already filled, work inside the form, wearing boots to protect clothing.

In areas around obstacles such as steps, position short form boards against the edge of the obstacle before the concrete is poured to ensure a correct level for tamping; remove these boards after tamping and fill in with concrete.

3 **Removing the inside form boards.** After pouring and levelling all of the concrete, remove the form assembly supporting the expansion-joint material inside the slab. To do this, build a bridge over the wet concrete by laying a ladder—topped with a scaffold board and supported by concrete blocks—across the outside form boards. Prise up the interior form boards and stakes with a crowbar, then fill the channels and stake holes with concrete. Level the fresh concrete with a short tamping beam, then remove the bridge.

4 **Floating the surface.** To compact and smooth the concrete, use a wooden skip float. First push the float forwards, tilting the front edge of the blade upwards, then draw it back, keeping the blade flat against the surface. Shovel fresh concrete into any remaining depressions, using a ladder bridge to reach areas beyond arm's length. Then skip-float the surface again.

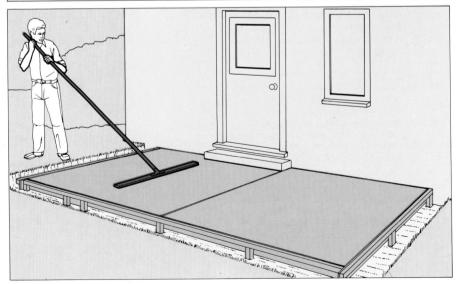

5 **Edging the concrete.** When the concrete is firm enough to hold a shape, run a bricklayer's trowel between the form boards and the outside edge of the slab to separate the top 25 mm of concrete from the wood *(below, left)*. Then push an edging tool back and forth along the cut *(below, right)*. Tilt the front of the tool slightly upwards when moving it backwards. Be careful not to gouge the concrete, since any deep indentations will be difficult to fill in later finishing steps.

Wait for the bleed water on the surface of the slab to evaporate before applying any of the finishes shown on the following pages.

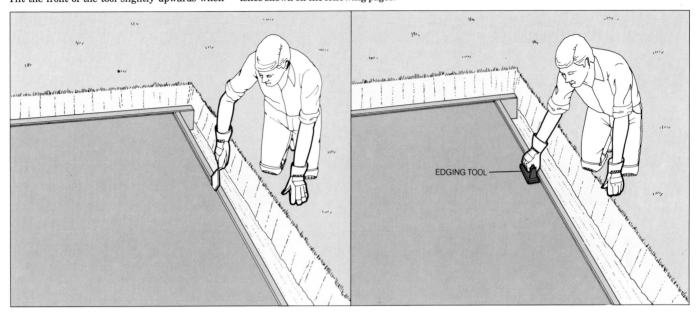

Finishing the Surface

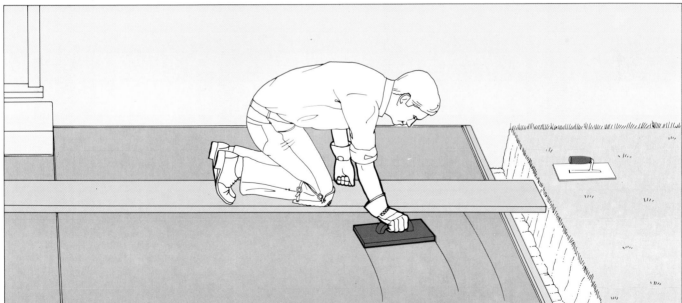

Trowelling a smooth finish. Kneeling on a scaffold board or wide plank laid over the slab, smooth the concrete with a wooden float, holding it flat and sweeping it in overlapping arcs across the whole surface. Move the bridge across the slab as you work over the surface.

Then go back over the entire slab with a rectangular steel trowel, tilting the trowel's leading edge slightly upwards. Work the surface until no concrete collects on the trowel, and the blade makes a ringing sound as you move it along the surface; this means that the concrete is too hard to work any further. Run the edging tool between the form boards and the edges of the slab as shown in the drawing at the top, right, to restore the edging lines.

Brooming on a skidproof surface. Wood-float the concrete *(page 19, below)*, but instead of steel-trowelling, draw a damp stiff-bristled broom across the surface. Either score straight lines at right angles to the forms or move the broom in arcs to produce a curved pattern. If the broom picks up small lumps of concrete, hose down the bristles to clean them and give the slab a few more minutes' drying time before you continue. If you have to press down hard to score the concrete, work fast; the concrete will soon be too hard to take a finish.

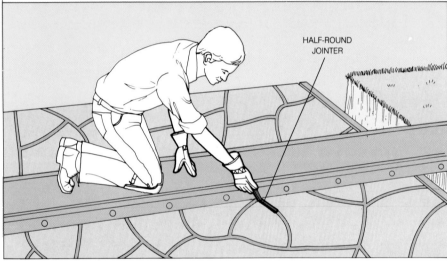

HALF-ROUND JOINTER

Creating a flagstone effect. After the bleed water has evaporated, skip-float the concrete, wood-float and steel-trowel, then score the surface with irregularly spaced grooves 6 to 15 mm deep, using a half-round jointer or a length of copper pipe bent into a flat S shape. Use a ladder bridge to reach inaccessible spots. After three or four hours, brush out the grooves with a dry paint-brush to remove any loose bits of concrete.

A Pebble-Aggregate Surface

1 **Preparing the surface.** Fill the forms with concrete *(page 17)*, but to the level of the top edge of the forms rather than above them. Tamp and level the concrete with a tamping beam notched so that its bottom edge is 10 mm below the top of the forms, then float the surface. Scatter an even layer of well-washed pebbles over the concrete and tap them just below the surface with a float. Then run a skip float across the surface, covering the stones with a thin, smooth layer of concrete.

2 **Exposing the aggregate.** After the bleed water has evaporated, brush the surface lightly with a stiff broom to expose the tops of the stones. Then, while a helper sprays the slab with water, brush it again, uncovering between a quarter and a half of the stones' circumference. If you dislodge any stones, stop brushing and wait until the concrete is a bit firmer before continuing. If the concrete is difficult to wash off, work quickly to expose the aggregate before the surface becomes too stiff.

Continue to spray the surface until the water runs clear and there is no noticeable cement film left on the aggregate. Clean individual spots missed in the general wash with a scrubbing brush. Between two and four hours after exposing the aggregate, wash and lightly brush the surface again to remove any cloudy residue from the stones.

Combining Hardwood with Concrete

1 **Installing hardwood rounds.** Paint 100 mm hardwood rounds top, sides and bottom with a generous coat of exterior-grade polyurethane varnish. Allow to dry, then place the rounds directly on the drainage bed in the desired pattern. Pour or shovel concrete carefully around each round. Level the concrete with a tamping beam. Smooth the surface with a darby—a metre-long board, 100 mm wide, with a short handle—instead of with a skip float. Hold the darby flat, and move it back and forth in a sawing motion to cut off bumps and fill in holes. Then run the darby over the slab a second time, sweeping it across the surface in broad arcs.

2 **Finishing the edges.** When the concrete is firm enough to hold a shape, run the end of a pointing trowel around the outside of each round to cut a 6 mm deep, V-shaped groove. Finish the slab with a wooden float and a trowel as on page 19.

Casting Concrete into Decorative Blocks

In addition to its role in walls and slabs cast as a single piece, poured concrete can be used to create individual concrete blocks in a wide variety of shapes, colours and textures. Especially appropriate for decorative structures such as garden paths, low walls and borders for flower beds, these ornamental blocks are usually cast in removable wooden moulds, although the concrete is sometimes poured directly into cavities scooped out of the earth, as on the opposite page.

Wooden moulds for ornamental blocks are made of prepared softwood and are set over a plywood base which can be covered with building paper, mould oil or polythene film to prevent the concrete from sticking. For easy removal, the moulds are hinged; if several blocks are to be cast at once, the moulds can be built in grid-like gangs *(opposite page, below)*.

The moulds are oiled and the concrete is poured, packed and levelled in much the same way as for a concrete slab *(pages 17–19)*. But the quantities of concrete involved in casting blocks are much smaller. You can mix the concrete yourself in a wheelbarrow or on a board, adding water to pre-mixed concrete or to a basic mix of 1 part cement, 2 parts sand and 3 parts coarse aggregate.

One way to give pattern and texture to hand-made blocks is to line the moulds with such materials as ridged rubber matting, polythene or strips of wood. However, be careful not to use a lining material with an undercut pattern that might interfere with removing the block from the mould. And in climates where alternate freezing and thawing occur, do not use patterns that act to collect rain; the expansion and contraction of trapped water would crumble the block's surface. To make sure that the concrete can flow into the crevices in the mould liner, use aggregate no more than 6 mm in diameter.

Many standard concrete mixtures produce surfaces that are decorative in themselves. For example, Portland cement can be acquired in white as well as the usual grey, and many suppliers offer the choice of different coloured sand—yellow, brown or white. In addition, there are decorative aggregates, such as polished pebbles and marble chips, that can create interesting built-in textures.

Other decorative surfaces can be produced by roughening the concrete. In one technique the surface of the block is layered to resemble travertine *(page 25)*; in another it is sprinkled with salt crystals that subsequently dissolve, leaving a pitted surface *(page 25)*. But since both these textures create traps for rainwater, they should not be used in areas where freezing and thawing are common.

Colour is added in the form of mineral-oxide pigments. Pre-coloured cement to use in the concrete mixture is available at builders' merchants. However, it is cheaper to add pigment to the cement yourself, and the colour choice is wider. Mineral oxides come in every basic colour, and they can be mixed together to create a wide variety of other hues. To achieve the clearest colours possible, use white cement, white sand and white aggregate.

Coloured concrete should be mixed in an automatic mixer, otherwise the results could be blotchy. Put the pigment in the mixer along with the cement and the aggregate, and blend them until the colour is uniform. Then add water as usual. The strength of the colour will, of course, depend on the proportion of pigment to cement. For a pastel colour, the proportions normally used are 1 or 2 parts of pigment to every 50 parts of cement; for deep shades, a good ratio is 1 part of pigment to every 20 parts of cement.

Always measure the ingredients by weight rather than volume, and never add more than 10 per cent pigment lest you weaken the concrete. If you are uncertain about the exact colour you want, make several small test batches, adding varying amounts or combinations of pigment to the dry mixture before putting in the water. Then allow these miniature blocks to cure for about a week; their colour will change slightly in curing. Be sure to keep a record of the ingredients you have used for each batch, so that you can duplicate the chosen colour exactly.

When adding either colour or decorative aggregate, one way to economize is to cast the blocks in two layers simultaneously, using pigment or aggregate in the top or face layer only. In making these tiered blocks, fill the form to within 25 mm of the top with ordinary concrete. Add the second layer, containing the pigment or aggregate, when the first layer is stiff enough to support it.

Another cost-saving alternative in using aggregate is to press the aggregate into the top of the concrete block *(pages 20–21)*. And the most economical way to apply colour to concrete is with a mixture called dry-shake: a combination of pigment, cement and sand that is sprinkled on top of the still-damp concrete block and floated in. You will need 1 kilogram of dry-shake for every 0.5 square metres of concrete. To get the coloured layer even, first sift about two-thirds of the mixture through your fingers on to the floated concrete surface. After several minutes, when the dry-shake mixture has absorbed some moisture from the concrete, smooth it with a float. Then sift on the rest of the dry-shake and trowel the surface smooth.

Moulds for Blocks from Earth and Wood

Earth forms for stepping stones. Working on site, dig holes 75 mm deep in the shapes of the blocks. Cut the edges with a spade or a garden trowel so that the perimeters are clean and as nearly vertical as possible. Pour and finish each stepping stone individually. Fill the hole with concrete, then tamp and smooth it with a wooden float, leaving the stone with a slightly rough but uniform texture.

When you are setting concrete stepping stones into a lawn, as shown here, it is best to make their top surfaces level with the surrounding earth, so that they will not interfere with convenient operation of a lawn mower.

Wooden forms for single blocks. Cut four pieces of timber for a frame. Mitre and hinge one frame corner. Butt-join the two adjacent corners; close the fourth with a hook and eye.

Set the frame on plywood; coat the plywood and frame with mould oil. Fill the mould, then tamp and level the concrete with a 100 by 50 mm board. Run a trowel between the concrete and the mould to compact the edges, then trowel the surface smooth. After 30 minutes, remove the frame, wash it with water, and repeat the process. Let the blocks cure for four days before moving them.

To make interlocking blocks, add removable inserts to a square frame: L-shaped pieces for a cruciform block; mitred corner pieces for a hexagon *(inset)*. For the blocks to fit together, all sides of the mould must be the same length.

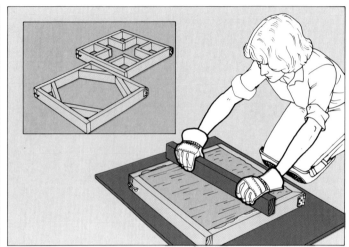

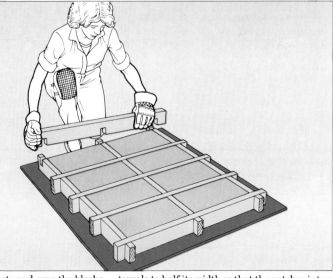

Ganged moulds for mass production. To cast multiple paving blocks on site, construct a rectangular frame of 75 by 50 mm boards. Assemble the frame so that its long sides extend 25 mm beyond each end, and nail 50 by 25 mm boards between the end extensions to make handles. Install 75 by 50 mm dividers inside the frame to define compartments of the desired shapes. Oil the mould, cast the concrete and cure the blocks as for an individual mould *(top, right)*, but tamp and level all the blocks at once by pulling a 100 by 50 mm board over their surface. Wait 30 minutes to an hour before removing the mould *(above, left)*. Reposition it and repeat the process.

To cast multiple building blocks, make a demountable grid of prepared timber notched at intervals to half its width so that the notches interlock. Position the notches to create the block shapes desired. Oil the mould sections before putting them together, and set the assembled mould on oiled plywood. Cast the blocks as described above. Wait 30 minutes before disassembling the mould *(above, right)*, then allow the blocks to cure for a week before using them.

Creating Patterns
with Mould Liners

Rubber matting. To model the surface of a concrete block with diagonal ridges, use skidproof rubber matting normally sold for doormats and stair treads. Coat the matting with mould oil and place it in the bottom of an oiled mould. Pour in a relatively wet mix of concrete, then tamp, level and cure the blocks as on page 23.

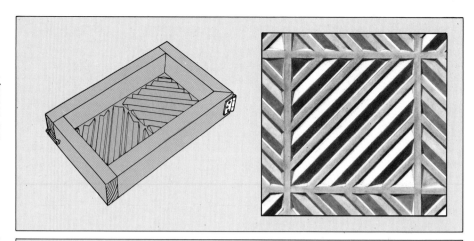

Embossing with gravel. To produce the dimpled surface shown on the right, place a sheet of household plastic film or other polythene film over a bed of smooth gravel. Use gravel of fairly uniform size and distribute it evenly over an area that matches the internal dimensions of the mould, leaving spaces between the individual stones. Then lay the film loosely over the gravel so that the weight of the concrete will force the film into the spaces. Position the oiled mould over the plastic, and pour and finish the concrete as described on page 23.

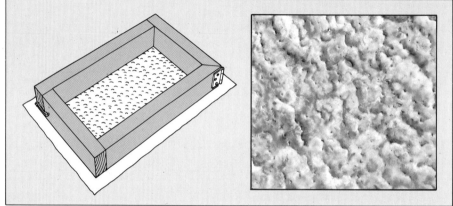

Wooden strips. To create a pattern of ridges and grooves, position strips of wood in the bottom of the mould. The edges of the wooden strips should be bevelled slightly, otherwise they may stick in the concrete. In the example on the right, the ridges in the finished block were roughened with a cold chisel. To cast variations, use half-round or triangular moulding, or arrange the wooden strips in a square. Coat the strips with mould oil before nailing them to the oiled base, and use concrete somewhat wetter than usual. Tamp it well so that it flows into the gaps between the strips.

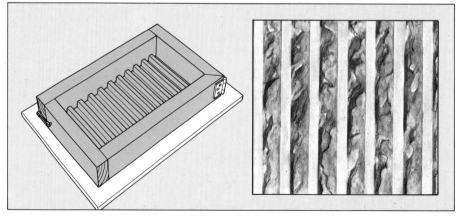

Wood-block dies. To add light and shadow to a plain concrete-block wall, intersperse blocks patterned with geometric bas-reliefs created with wood-block dies. In this example, triangular dies are placed in the corners of the oiled mould to form dramatic trapezium shapes. When using dies with exposed end-grain, be sure to sand the end-grain smooth so that the dies slip easily from the finished concrete blocks. If the pattern is raised, as here, deepen the mould by the depth of the dies to bring the recessed areas level with the surrounding wall. Oil the dies before fixing them in the mould, then cast and finish the concrete as described on page 23.

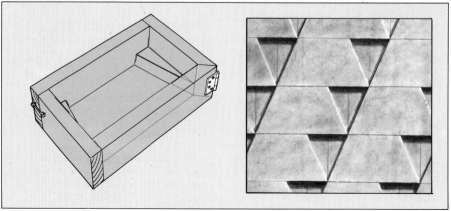

Roughened Surfaces for Textural Interest

Exposed aggregate. To bring decorative aggregate into relief, wash a thin layer of concrete from the top of the block. First, finish the block through the trowelling stage *(page 23)*, and let it set until the aggregate is firmly anchored but the concrete is still soluble—about an hour. Then, with a garden hose and a stiff brush, simultaneously flush and scrub the top of the block until the top of the aggregate is exposed. Test a corner of the block first to see if brushing tends to dislodge the aggregate.

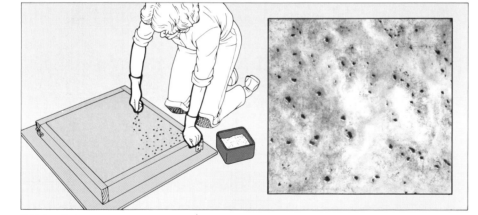

Pebbled paving. To add a veneer of pebbled paving to a plain concrete block, fill the oiled mould with concrete to within 5 mm of the top. Level the surface with a 100 by 50 mm board, notched 5 mm deep at the ends to fit over the edges of the mould. Then wet down the pebbles or stones of the aggregate, and distribute them in a single layer over the concrete. Press the aggregate into the concrete with a float until it is buried just below the surface. When the concrete is set but the cement is still soluble, flush and brush the surface as above to reveal the top of the pebbles.

A salt-pitted surface. To create a pitted surface in the concrete, scatter large grains of rock salt over the block while it is still damp—just after it has been floated or trowelled smooth. Press the salt crystals into the concrete with a float, but do not bury them. Allow the block to cure, then wash away any undissolved salt with a garden hose. Wear rubber gloves in case the salt dries or irritates the skin of your hands.

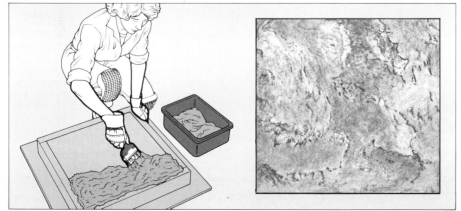

A travertine finish. To add the rough, streaked look of travertine to concrete block, tamp the surface to compact it, but float it only lightly so that the concrete retains a rough surface. Then use a stiff brush to dab on mortar made of 1 part cement to 2 parts sand, coating the concrete with an uneven, patchy surface with ridges up to 5 mm high. When the water sheen disappears, float or trowel off the tops of the ridges, leaving both mortar and concrete rough in the crevices between. To heighten the streaked look, you may tint the mortar topping with mineral-oxide pigment *(page 22)* before you put it on the concrete.

Steps Designed for Flat and Sloping Sites

Steps faced with a decorative veneer of brick, stone or tiles provide a handsome link between patio and house or between patio and lawn. They can be built in various ways, depending on the site or on design considerations. Some steps are solid concrete; some, on sloping sites, use the ground for support, with or without concrete footings to anchor the risers. Steps may descend on to a patio at right angles to the house or, where space is limited, they can approach it laterally, hugging the house wall. Finally, the treads can be curved instead of straight, adding an extra design element to the patio area.

Steps made of solid concrete are poured into a wooden form, and have a concrete base that extends at least 100 mm below ground level. Steps cut into a sloping site vary in structural needs. In mild climates, where freezing and thawing do not occur to shift the ground, steps can simply be bolstered with rocks, railway sleepers or logs as risers. Otherwise, the risers are best anchored in a narrow concrete footing, with a gravel bed beneath the treads for drainage.

Concrete steps over a metre high may have to be tied to the foundation with re-inforcing bars; in this case, seek expert advice. Also, the top of the steps should be below the house's damp-proof course— situated in most houses just below the door threshold. For long flights of steps, you can save on concrete by stacking hollow concrete blocks filled with hardcore or gravel in the wooden form to within 150 mm of the sides and top of the form. Allow for a full 150 mm of concrete over this concrete-block base, however, or the stairs will be too weak.

Outdoor steps need deeper treads and shallower risers than indoor steps, for good

Making Forms for Straight and Curved Treads

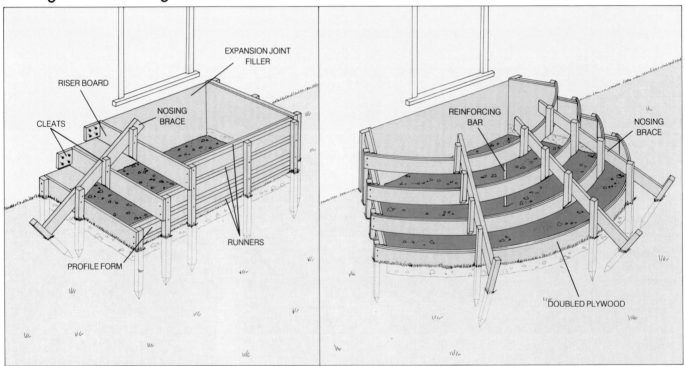

Planning the forms. Dig a hole 100 mm deep and the dimensions of the base of the steps. For straight steps *(above, left)*, cut out the profile form and nail to it 50 by 50 mm runners top and bottom as well as along the length of the form at the height of the tread of each step. The bottom of the form rests on the ground and is supported on each side by 50 by 50 mm stakes, by additional stakes running flush with the risers of each step, and by a stake at the middle of the landing. The back of the form is supported top and bottom by runners, a stake at the outside corner, and another in the corner near the house wall, where it is nailed temporarily to the wall. The riser boards

are nailed to the outside vertical stakes and to cleats which have been nailed or screwed to the house wall; the riser board for the bottom step has stakes at each end. Additional support for the risers is provided by a 100 by 50 mm nosing brace which is wedged against a stake driven into the ground and secured to vertical cleats nailed to the riser boards. The cleats and the bottoms of the boards are bevelled to admit a steel float for finishing the treads.

For curved steps *(above, right)*, the side profile forms, braced with runners and stakes, diverge to create concentric steps and risers of different lengths. Determine their lengths by nailing in

position the bottom riser boards made from flexible 9 or 12 mm plywood. When the curve of the riser board is right, nail another piece of ply over it for additional strength. Follow the curve of the bottom board in making successive boards, checking with a measure that the distance from the previous board remains constant. Reinforce all riser boards with an additional piece of plywood. Install nosing braces as for straight steps, cutting them off vertically just beyond the top riser board. Wedge a length of reinforcing bar under the top board (this can be left in place after concreting). For both straight and curved steps, install expansion joint filler against the house wall.

footing and maximum visibility in all weather and all degrees of light. The treads should be at least 220 mm deep and the risers between 75 and 220 mm high; the total measurement of two treads plus one riser should come to between 550 and 700 mm. In addition, the landing and each tread should be sloped downwards by 6 mm in every 300 mm to allow rainwater to run off. A good side-to-side measurement is 1200 mm; the landing should be at least as wide as the steps, and not less than 400 mm longer than the width of the door, to provide an area for entering and leaving the house safely.

Check local building regulations for other requirements that may apply, and plan the dimensions of the steps. Level the ground below the door where the steps will be, and measure from the ground to the planned height of the landing. Divide this measurement—the total rise—by the intended rise of a single step to find the number of steps required. Thus, if the rise comes to 450 mm, you could make three steps, each with a 150 mm riser. However, make sure that the angle of pitch—the angle between the ground level and a notional line connecting the front edges of all the treads—is not greater than 42 degrees.

From your plan, lay out the profile of the steps on a sheet of 18 mm shuttering ply, taking into account the drainage slope and also the thickness of any materials you in-tend to veneer the steps with—brick, tiles or stone (pages 39, 46 and 49)—plus the mortar in which they will be set. The height of the form is the same as the total rise of the steps.

Railings should be installed on all steps narrower than 1 metre and higher than 600 mm. The railings should be 900 mm high on landings and, measured vertically from the pitch line, 840 mm on flights of steps. The sturdiest railings rest on solid-steel posts sunk into holes in the concrete and held in place with epoxy resin. You can order custom-made railings from a metal-works, or have steel posts cut and drilled at a metalworks and build the sturdy steel and wood railing shown on page 28.

Pouring and Finishing Built-Up Steps

1 Filling the form. Coat the inside of the form with mould oil, then fill the form with concrete blocks and hardcore to within 150 mm of the sides and top. Fill in the remaining space with a stiff mix of concrete; use a shovel to compact the concrete, or a hired vibrator poker to eliminate air pockets. Tamp the landing and treads. Set 75 mm-diameter cylinders of plastic or polystyrene 100 mm into the wet concrete to make holes for the railing posts.

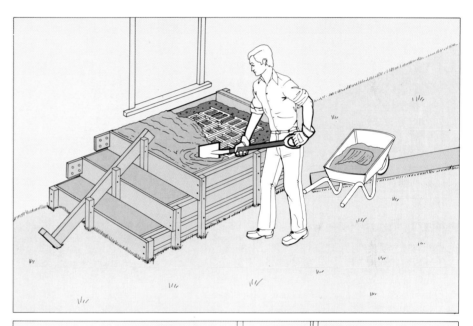

2 Smoothing the surface. Leave the concrete to set for about 15 minutes, then finish the treads and landing with a steel trowel. Carefully detach the riser boards and finish the risers. Finish the inside corners of the treads and their outer nosings with inside and outside-step tools (inset). For a non-skid finish, sprinkle grains of aluminium oxide or silicon carbide on the landing and treads, and work them in with a steel trowel. Leave the side and back sections of the form in place for a week, and keep the concrete covered with poly-thene to cure it. When these sections are removed, chip away small projections with a cold chisel, and fill depressions and smooth the surface with quick-setting patching cement laid on with a pointing trowel.

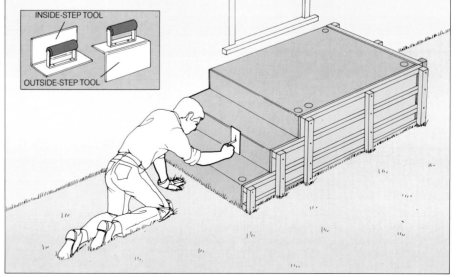

INSIDE-STEP TOOL

OUTSIDE-STEP TOOL

A Custom Railing of Steel and Wood

A railing set in concrete. The support posts for this railing are 25 mm square hollow steel bars. The handrails and guard rails are made of 100 by 37 mm hardwood with rounded edges sanded smooth, and coated with sealer and finish. The handrails and guard rails are spaced with no more than 100 mm between them and they are secured to the outside of the posts with 6 mm galvanized coach bolts in countersunk holes.

The posts may be set in holes cast in the concrete *(page 27, Step 1)*, or post holes may be drilled into the masonry after the steps are completed; the posts are secured with epoxy resin. At the top of the flight of steps two posts are set side by side with a space of 40 mm between them. The ends of the handrail and guard rails for the steps are mitre-cut at an angle of 90 degrees less the angle of pitch of the steps; once secured, their top ends are planed flush with the horizontal landing handrail and guard rails *(inset)*.

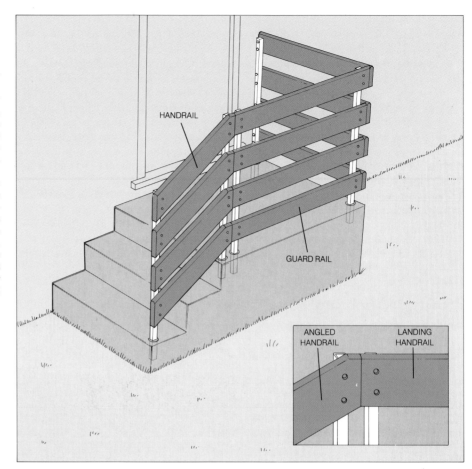

HANDRAIL

GUARD RAIL

ANGLED HANDRAIL

LANDING HANDRAIL

Building In-Ground Steps

1 Preparing the ground. Drive in two short stakes at the top of the slope on each side of the planned steps, then drive in two corresponding long stakes at the bottom of the slope. Mark the height of the top tread in the short stakes. With a line level and string stretched taut between the short and long stakes, determine the total rise and the total run of the steps *(inset)*. Work out the number of steps by the method described on page 27, reckoning on an ideal riser height of 150 mm, and mark the height of each riser on the lower stakes. Smooth the area and tie strings as a slope guide from the marks on the short stakes to the bottoms of the long stakes.

Establish the line of the bottom step by measuring horizontally from the bottom stakes the depth of the tread plus the thickness of the riser material. Cut a vertical wall to the height of the first mark on the lower stakes less the thickness of the tread material, then level the ground up to this cut. Make all successive treads and risers to the same dimensions, checking the level of the steps against the marks on the lower stakes and using the slope guides as a reference.

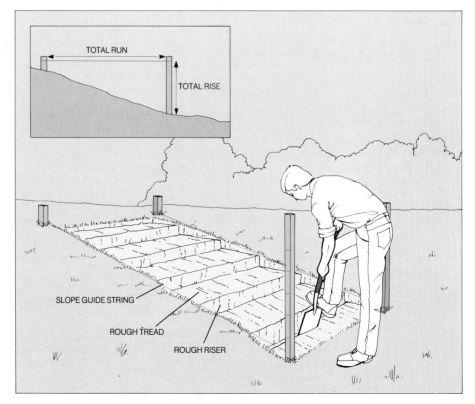

TOTAL RUN

TOTAL RISE

SLOPE GUIDE STRING

ROUGH TREAD

ROUGH RISER

2 **Setting the riser bricks in concrete.** To anchor the risers—in this example using bricks on end—dig a trench 220 mm deep and 100 mm wide along the base of each rough riser. Mix a batch of concrete, and fill the footing trench for the bottom riser. Set the riser bricks in the concrete, flush against the rough riser and extending 50 mm higher than the rough tread above. Use the slope guide as a reference and a level to align the tops of the bricks with the marks on the lower stakes, allowing for the thickness of the tread material. Set riser bricks in the remaining trenches in the same way. When you reach behind the top rough tread, set a row of bricks to a height that will allow the tread to slope down by 6 mm per 300 mm to the next riser below. Allow the concrete to set for at least 24 hours.

RISER BRICKS

3 **Finishing the steps.** Backfill the rough treads with washed gravel to the top of the riser bricks, and then tamp the gravel down and establish a drainage slope, 6 mm per 300 mm, from the back to the front of each tread. Build treads, starting at the bottom step, by mortaring the tread material—flagstone in this example—to the riser. Allow the tread to overlap the riser by 20 mm, to create an overhanging nosing that makes the steps easier to see at dusk *(inset)*.

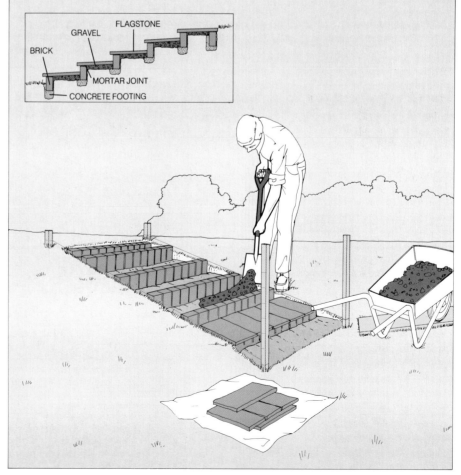

FLAGSTONE

GRAVEL

BRICK

MORTAR JOINT

CONCRETE FOOTING

Removing the Flaws from Existing Paving

A new veneer of brick, tiles or stone can do wonders for an old concrete slab or flight of steps, turning it from an eyesore into an ornament. But before veneering can begin, the worn concrete needs some preliminary testing and may need to be reconditioned. First, check a slab to see it has the proper gradient for good drainage and make sure that a slab or a flight of steps is structurally sound. Then you may need to make good the surface of the concrete to remove any irregularities.

To test the soundness of concrete, drop a metal bar in several places. A sharp, ringing noise indicates that the concrete is solid; a dull thud signals crumbling beneath the surface. If crumbling has occurred, the slab or steps will have to be rebuilt. Break up the concrete with a sledge hammer or a hired pneumatic hammer, and use the rubble as a base for a new concrete structure *(page 8)*.

To test the gradient, spray the surface with a hose. If most of the water settles in puddles or runs towards the house, the slab is badly graded. In this case, too, it is best to break up the slab and start again. Accumulated water will eventually weaken the mortar that bonds the veneer brick, tiles or stone to the concrete.

Less serious surface flaws are more easily corrected. Minor cracks or small holes may have formed with wear and age. You may also find high spots or bumps left by careless construction. Most of these imperfections can be fixed with a few basic tools. Use a cold chisel and a club hammer to remove damaged concrete, a trowel and a wooden float for patching. Always wear protective goggles and gloves when you are chiselling concrete.

Remove any old paint with a commercial stripper, then look for high spots by drawing a metal straightedge over the surface of the concrete. Any bump that protrudes 3 mm or more should be cut down with a mason's rubbing brick or an electric drill fitted with a silicon carbide wheel, both of which can be obtained from builders' merchants. If you encounter an irregularity covering an area of more than 300 square millimetres, it is best to break up the surface with a cold chisel and fill it in as you would a large depression.

Small surface cracks and holes less than 25 mm deep can be filled with latex or epoxy patching mortars that are made especially for this purpose and that bond far better than ordinary patching filler. The epoxy compounds are slightly stronger and have greater water resistance than the latex ones.

For larger holes or many small ones, where special compounds might be too expensive to use, chisel out the damaged concrete and trowel in an ordinary patching filler—a packaged mixture of cement and sand in a 1:4 ratio. If you brush the damaged area with an epoxy or acrylic bonding adhesive before adding the filler, the patch will adhere more securely. Chipped corners can also be restored in this way, as shown on the opposite page.

When the smoothed surface is ready for veneering, remove dust and debris with a wire brush; apply a commercial concrete cleaner to remove oil, grease or other stains; and rinse with water. Then attach the bricks, tiles or stones as for a newly constructed slab *(pages 32, 40 and 47)*.

Making a Concrete Patch

1 **Preparing the damaged area.** Chip out the concrete in the damaged area with a cold chisel and a club hammer. The hole should be 40 mm deep, the edge undercut slightly so that the bottom of the depression is wider than the top *(inset)*. Clear away the concrete rubble with a brush, and wash out the area with a hose. Blot up excess water with a sponge.

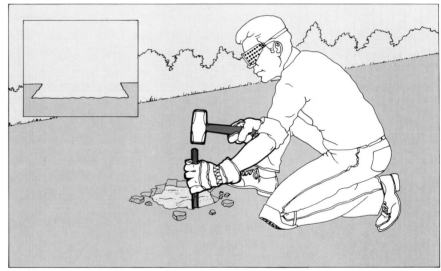

2 **Adding the adhesive and filler.** Spread bonding adhesive in the cavity with a stiff-bristled brush, such as one commonly used for dusting before exterior painting. Cover the area completely with an even coat, then wipe up spills round the edge of the hole with a rag. Check the manufacturer's drying time instructions—usually about 30 minutes to two hours.

Prepare the cement-and-sand filler according to the manufacturer's instructions, and trowel the mixture into the hole before the bonding adhesive loses its tackiness.

3 **Smoothing the patch.** With the patch in place, level the surface by drawing a wooden float back and forth across it several times. Lift excess filler around the edges of the patch with a trowel; then, before the patch hardens, wipe the edge joint smooth with a rag. Cover the patch with a sheet of polythene for five to seven days, until the patch has cured completely.

Rebuilding a Crumbling Step Corner

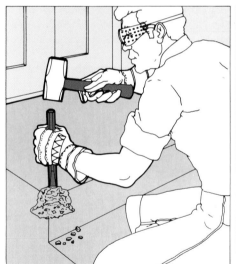

1 **Preparing the corner for a patch.** Chisel away a crumbling corner of a step until you reach solid concrete on all sides, then flatten the bottom of the cavity and undercut the sides slightly.

Cut two form boards from 18 mm plywood to surround the corner and contain the filler. The width of the form boards should match the height of the step riser. To steady the boards, cut a 50 by 50 mm support stake; the length of the stake will depend on the height of the damaged step above the ground.

When you are ready to fill the corner, brush away any rubble and paint the cavity with a coat of bonding (*opposite page, Step 2*).

2 **Filling in the corner.** While the adhesive is still tacky, coat the inside faces of the form boards with mould oil and nail them in place around the corner. Support the front board with bricks. Before the adhesive hardens (follow the manufacturer's instructions, usually 30 minutes to two hours), trowel the cement-and-sand patching filler in (*Step 3, above*) and tamp it down to fill the entire hole. As the patch begins to harden, level the surface with a wooden float and cut away any excess filler. Cover with a sheet of polythene for five to seven days.

Brick Patterns to Set in Sand or Cement

Brick has been used for centuries to surface public squares, roads and paths throughout much of the world. The qualities that make it suitable for these uses make brick a good choice for a patio surface that is at once elegant and practical. A brick surface is enduring, weather resistant and low-glare, and it is composed of small standard units that are simple to install and easy to maintain.

Durable enough to use on driveways, brick makes an attractive low-cost veneer for a concrete-slab patio. Alternatively, it can be laid without mortar, over sand and lime—an underlay that has certain advantages. The lime, which is mixed in a 1:6 ratio with sand, stabilizes the mixture but allows for some movement as the base fractures and then resets with freezing and thawing. Such a base allows rainwater to seep down to tree or shrub roots; in addition, bricks can be removed in order to accommodate a broadening tree trunk or an additional flower bed.

Many brick-like blocks used today are not the traditional clay bricks baked in the sun or fired in an oven, but are made of moulded concrete. For this reason, the popular reddish-brown rectangular brick is only one of a wide array of colours and shapes. A variety of surface textures are also available. The best paving materials are relatively smooth, because a rough or grooved surface collects rainwater; if the water freezes, the bricks may crack. But avoid bricks that are glazed or so smooth that they become slippery when wet. In a climate where the ground freezes, use engineering-quality bricks, which are able to withstand severe weather conditions.

The dimensions of paving materials also vary widely: they can be as thin as 32 mm or as thick as 80 mm, and they range in length from 200 to 450 mm and in width from 100 to 225 mm. This range of sizes allows you to plan a patio with or without gaps between the bricks. For a pattern laid tight on sand and lime you will need special paving bricks, exactly half as wide as they are long.

Facing bricks and engineering bricks are sized to accommodate a 10 mm gap for mortar—a gap that not only accentuates the pattern but serves to channel off rainwater down the long side of the brick. (To take advantage of this function, you can orient the pattern to carry water down the slope of the patio, away from the house.) For patterns set in mortar, you will need fewer bricks—5½ bricks per square metre less than for patterns set tight in sand.

A sand-lime bed should start far enough from the base of a tree for the bricks to lie level. The composition of a sand-lime bed depends on how well the underlying soil drains. Usually a 50 mm sand-lime base on well-tamped earth is sufficient, but you may need a 100 mm layer of washed gravel under the sand if you live in an area where rainfall is heavy or where the soil is hard-packed clay. If drainage is a particular problem, slope the bed about 25 mm every 1.5 to 2 metres. You can also lay a perforated pipe of clay, plastic or bitumen in the gravel layer to drain water away from wet spots.

Bricks laid in sand and lime must be contained by a permanent edging, to check horizontal shifts. The edging is usually set at soil level, or 50 mm above the soil at the edge of a flower bed.

You can further limit shifting by filling the joints between bricks with a mixture of cement and sand, brushed in dry and then misted with water. Use a mixture of 1 part cement to 6 parts sand, and keep the patio damp for three days. To avoid staining the brick, remove all traces of cement from the surface before misting, and do not attempt dry cement filling during wet weather. A thin coat of silicone brick sealer, applied to the brick with a paint roller before you sweep in the cement mixture, will help to prevent staining.

Weed growth in a sand-lime bed can be checked by a vapour barrier of perforated roofing felt or plastic sheeting directly below the sand and lime, but herbicides or weeding may be needed to rid cracks of all unwanted plants. Be careful not to use weedkillers close to trees and any other desirable plants.

The moss that grows between bricks in shady areas can be attractive, but on the patio surface it can be a slippery hazard; if necessary, you can remove it with a strong fungicide sold at garden centres. In damp areas, bricks are sometimes discoloured by mould; you can remove it by scrubbing the bricks with household bleach.

If weeds are a problem—or if a stronger, more permanent patio is wanted—bricks can be set in mortar on a concrete slab. Prepare the slab as shown on pages 8–14 and 17–19, to ensure a good bond between brick and concrete. The best mix of mortar for outdoor use is 1 part cement to 5 parts sand, with plasticizer added to the water according to the manufacturer's instructions. Use builders' sand, not sharp sand which makes the mortar difficult to mix. The mortar should be just soft enough to slide easily off the shovel. In hot and dry weather, dampen the bricks thoroughly before applying mortar, and always wear gloves to protect your hands from irritants in the mortar.

A mortared brick surface will usually benefit from having an edging which will protect and hide the edges of the concrete slab. Set such a border before surfacing the slab, so that the border will serve as a reference level for the surface bricks. If the slab has expansion joints, matching joints are required in the brick veneer. Fill the expansion joint between bricks with expansion joint filler; cover the filler with self-levelling polysulphide or silicone caulk.

Bricks used for paving. Of the thousands of sizes, shapes and shades available in bricks and brick-like blocks, those used for paving fall into three categories: facing bricks, paving bricks and interlocking pavers. Facing bricks *(below, top)* used for paving should be of the dense-faced variety rather than the porous type. They come in a wide range of colours and measure 215 by 102.5 by 65 mm to accommodate 10 mm joints. Paving bricks *(below, centre)* are more durable and often more expensive than facing bricks, with widths exactly half their lengths to fit mortarless patterns. Interlocking pavers *(below, bottom)*, usually made of concrete, are defined by their shape. When pavers are combined in a pattern, each one locks its neighbour in place, preventing shifting.

Primary paving patterns. These four patterns can be used as shown or in combination to give a variety of surface designs. Bricks laid in rows for a stack bond pattern *(below, top)* are difficult to align over a large area, but a row of stack bond is often used to frame another pattern. In a variation—stretcher bond *(below, centre)*—the bricks are staggered by half their length. It is an easy, all-purpose pattern, laid with or without mortar. Two locking patterns, herringbone *(second from bottom)* and basketweave *(bottom)*, increase the durability of a mortarless patio; each pair of bricks is held in place by a pair of bricks at right angles to it. Herringbone can be laid diagonally, to direct a viewer's eye in a certain direction. To vary any of these designs, set the bricks on their sides, three to a square, for a tighter pattern.

Two designs for added drama. A circular patio *(below, top)* around a tree, statue or fountain emphasizes the object you wish to feature. Beginning with two circles of half-bricks—full bricks would leave unsightly spaces if laid in a tight circle—the pattern radiates outwards.

The scalloped pattern *(below, bottom)*, often used on European boulevards, adds a graceful touch to a patio. Rows of bricked arcs enclose scalloped spaces filled with whole and cut bricks.

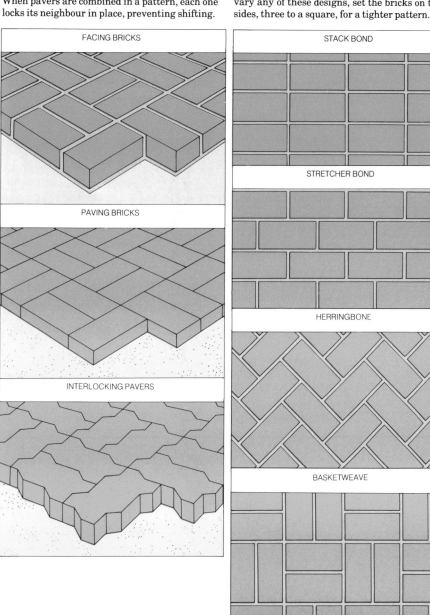

FACING BRICKS

PAVING BRICKS

INTERLOCKING PAVERS

STACK BOND

STRETCHER BOND

HERRINGBONE

BASKETWEAVE

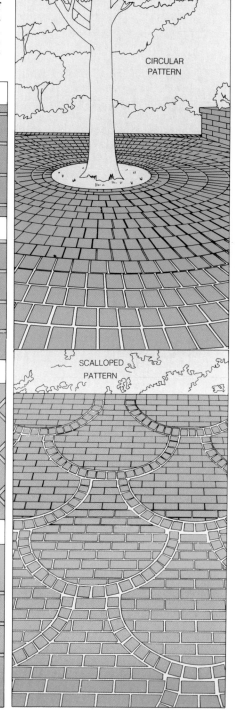

CIRCULAR PATTERN

SCALLOPED PATTERN

Laying Bricks on a Bed of Sand and Lime

Setting edging brick. Establish the edges of the patio with pegs and string *(page 9)*, then dig a bed for the bricks and sand-lime base. If the patio adjoins a house wall, the drainage bed will have to be graded *(page 10)*. To avoid unnecessary brick cutting, first do a test run with the bricks that will form the edging and, inside them, a row of bricks that will form the surface of the patio. Adjust the perimeter of the patio to incorporate as many whole bricks as possible, remove the test bricks and, using a square-edged spade, dig a trench about 100 mm wide and 180 mm below the original soil level, just inside the edges of the bed. Trowel in a 30 mm layer of sand-lime mix and set bricks upright in the trench. For a more solid edging, use a layer of stiff mortar mixed in a 1:6 ratio in the bottom of the trench. Tamp earth against the bricks to hold them vertical, the top edges touching the string guide. Where the patio adjoins a flower bed, let the edging rise 50 mm above where the paved surface will be. Use the reference strings to align the border bricks with each other as well.

To make a saw-tooth pattern with teeth protruding 50 mm above the surface *(inset, below, left)*, set the bricks at an angle of 45 degrees in the trench. Other choices for edgings include treated 150 by 50 mm hardwood boards *(inset, below, centre)* set in a narrower trench and fastened at the corners with galvanized angle brackets; or upright bricks set in a curve *(inset, below, right)* for a rounded corner. To lay out a curved corner, use a level to align the tops of the bricks. Flatten the earth inside the bed with a tamper *(page 10)*, add washed gravel and a vapour barrier if necessary, then spread a 50 mm layer of sand-lime over the bed. Smooth and level the sand with a screed rail, then tamp the surface thoroughly again.

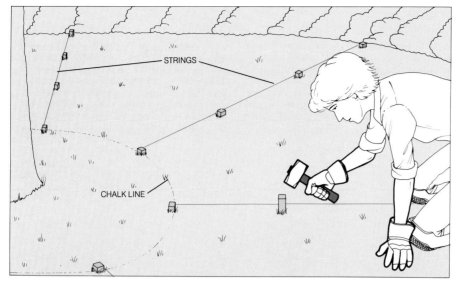

A Circular Patio to Surround a Tree

1 Establishing the level. From hardboard or cardboard make a circular template that, cut in half and with its centred removed, will fit around the tree. To avoid wide gaps between the half-bricks in the first two circles, the diameter of the template must be not less than 900 mm. Mark round the template with chalk or lime, then remove the template. Just inside the marked circle, drive in a ring of pegs to the planned height of the patio at intervals not greater than 300 mm. From these pegs, run strings radiating to temporary pegs beyond the area to be paved, creating equal segments. Adjust the strings to allow for a slight drainage slope. Drive in pegs at 500 mm intervals along these strings, their tops level with the strings. Remove the temporary pegs and strings.

2 Laying the inner circle. Excavate the area to the depth of the bricks plus the depth of the sand-lime bed, and level the floor of the excavation using the pegs as guides. Now install the edging *(opposite page)* and lay a 50 mm sand-lime bed. Working outwards from the inner rim of the excavated area, lay two circles of half-bricks, adjusting the gaps between them to avoid cutting any bricks. Tap the bricks into place with a club hammer and a timber straightedge, adding or removing sand-lime as necessary. Check the level of the bricks using the peg tops as a reference.

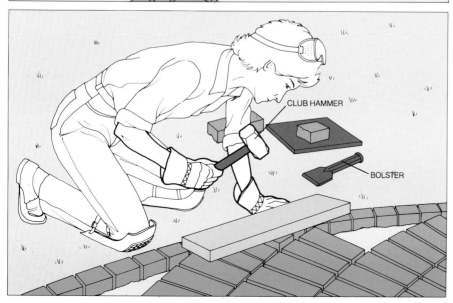

3 Completing the patio. Lay the rest of the area with full bricks, a circle at a time. Use the pegs as guides to maintain the regularity of the pattern and to check the level of each brick as you lay it; remove the pegs as you overtake them. Wearing goggles, cut bricks to fill the final spaces against the edging with a bolster and club hammer *(page 36)*. With a stiff-bristled brush, spread the area with a layer of sand-lime; then, with a soft brush, sweep diagonally across the bricks to fill the joints. Sprinkle the patio with a fine spray of water to settle the sand-lime in the joints, repeating the process if necessary when the patio has completely dried out.

A Choice of Methods for Cutting Bricks

Using a bolster or angle grinder. To cut a small number of bricks, use a wide chisel—called a bolster—and a small club hammer *(below, left)*. To cut many bricks, score them with an angle grinder equipped with a carbide masonry blade *(below, right)*, and use a club hammer to break them. If you are using a bolster, cushion the brick on sand or a board, and score it along the cutting line on all four sides with sharp taps on the tool. To break the brick, position the bolster upright on the cutting line and give it a hard blow with the club hammer.

To do the scoring with an angle grinder, hold the brick in a simple jig made of four 50 by 50 mm timber scraps spaced a brick's width and a brick's length apart and nailed to a piece of ply-wood, and slowly guide the blade along the cutting line to groove the brick. Turn the brick over and make a matching groove on the other side. Then remove the brick and tap the underside along the groove to split it in two. If the brick does not split cleanly, use the chisel end of a brick hammer *(inset, below)* to chip off the excess. Wear gloves and goggles whenever you cut brick.

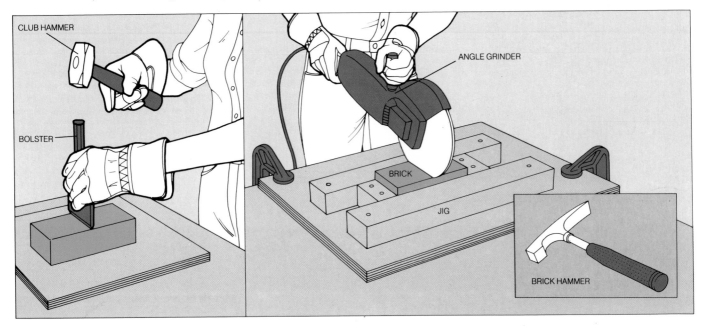

CLUB HAMMER

BOLSTER

ANGLE GRINDER

BRICK

JIG

BRICK HAMMER

Laying a Herringbone Patio

Using a string guide. Stretch a string across the centre of the patio, holding it in place with bricks set just outside the edging. Using paving bricks exactly twice as long as they are wide, begin laying bricks in the pattern and order indicated *(right)* on either side of the string; locating the centre point of each header under the string ensures that the bricks are set at an exact 45-degree angle to the string. Continue the double line to the other edge of the patio, tapping the bricks in place with a club hammer cushioned by a piece of scrap timber. Check that the bricks are evenly butted together and that they are level. Move the string to provide a reference for the next double row of bricks, and continue until the remaining parts of the patio are laid with full bricks. Use cut bricks at the edges, then sweep sand-lime into all the cracks.

GUIDE STRING

Setting Bricks in Overlapping Scallops

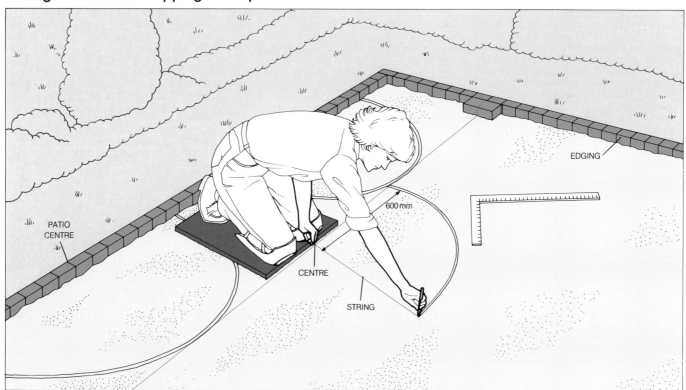

1 Scribing scallop arcs. Starting from the centre of one end of an edged sand-lime bed, scribe semi-circles with a string-and-nail compass. Give each arc a radius of 600 mm, locating the centres 1500 mm apart so that there is a 300 mm space between each arc.

After scribing the first row of arcs, with partial arcs at the sides if necessary, stretch a string between two bricks across the tops of the arcs to establish a baseline for the next row of arcs. Scribe another row of arcs, positioned with their centres at the halfway points between the arcs in the first row *(above)*; use a 600 mm steel square to locate each new centre. Kneel on boards to avoid disturbing the arcs you have already scribed. Continue until you have filled the area, using partial arcs at the far edge if necessary.

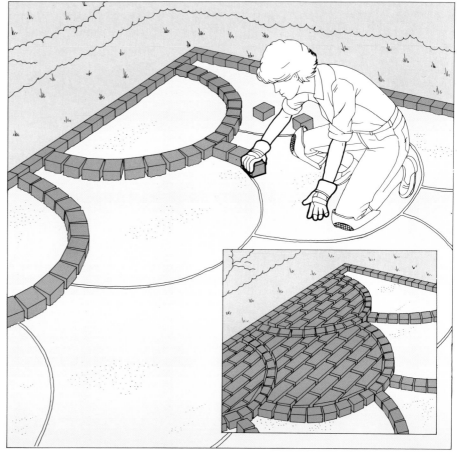

2 Filling the scallops. Line the outside of each scribed arc with half-bricks, using about 17 bricks for each arc in the first row and 15 or 16 bricks for each arc in the succeeding rows. Then lay parallel rows of cut and full bricks to fill each scalloped arc, allowing a 10 mm gap between bricks. Sweep sand-lime into the gaps.

A Brick Veneer
for a Concrete Slab

1 **Setting brick in mortar.** Using the methods described on page 34, lay a brick edging set in mortar around the perimeter of the concrete slab. The edging should be the depth of a brick plus 10 mm above the surface of the slab. Leave the edging to set for 48 hours.

Working from a corner of the slab, lay a bed of mortar four bricks long, 100 mm wide and 15 mm deep. Place the corner brick in position, using a 10 mm plywood spacer to keep the gap between the edging and the brick uniform. Tap the brick into position with the handle of your trowel. Lay the next three bricks in the same line, put down a new four-brick-long mortar bed, and continue to the other side of the patio. Use a spacer to ensure regular gaps between the bricks. To keep the rows of bricks level and in line, use a taut line strung between bricks set outside the edging. Fill any gaps in the patio with cut bricks, and allow at least 24 hours before walking on the patio surface.

EDGING

GUIDE STRING

SPACER

MORTAR BED

2 **Filling gaps with mortar.** Allow the mortared bricks to dry for 48 hours. Fill the gaps between bricks by trowelling in a wet mortar mixed to a stiff paste *(right)*; alternatively, brush in a dry mortar of 1 part cement to 3 parts sand, then sprinkle with a fine spray of water. Finish the wet mortar either flush or concave with a trowel or jointer; the dry mortar mix may need a second application as the water causes settlement.

After about an hour, when the mortar is stiff but not solid, clean off any stains on the bricks with a sponge and water. If staining is bad, use a brick-cleaning fluid once the mortar has cured. Cover the brickwork for a minimum of 24 hours.

JOINTER

Covering Steps with Bricks

Regular paving bricks provide an attractive alternative to quarry tiles or flagstones for veneering steps, particularly when they match a brick patio in colour and pattern. Custom-made bricks with rounded nosings can be used to cover the treads, but a straight edge to the treads, with no overhang, reduces the danger of slipping on the steps.

If you plan to build a form to pour the concrete core yourself *(pages 26–27)*, design it so that standard 215 by 102.5 by 65 mm bricks will cover the core with a minimum of cutting. Take care to plan the risers so they are covered by whole bricks.

No matter how thin a veneer you put over existing concrete steps, the bottom riser will be higher than the rest. To compensate, you can build a path leading to the steps. If you start from scratch, make the first step shallower than the others by the thickness of a tread brick.

In either case, you will need to add a footing of poured concrete 150 mm wide and 300 mm deep around the step core to support the brick veneer on the sides and the first riser. Finish the surface of the footing 75 mm below ground level.

The best mortar mix for veneering steps is 1 part cement to 5 or 6 parts sand. Mix only small quantities of mortar at a time, no more than will be used in 30 minutes. In hot weather, it may be necessary to dampen both concrete and bricks before mortaring, to ensure proper adhesion. Expansion joints are needed where a stair landing meets a door threshold, and where a brick patio or path meets the sides or front of the brick veneer.

1 **Encasing the step sides.** Starting at the front of the bottom riser, lay a course of bricks below ground level projecting the width of a brick plus a mortar joint at each side. Then lay bricks along the sides of the steps, starting at the front of the steps so that any cut bricks will occur next to the house wall. Start the second course with a full brick at each corner, header towards the front. Fill in the front of the riser with whole bricks and finish off the sides. Repeat the stretcher bond pattern *(page 33)* for the next two courses. Start the fifth course with bricks at each corner of the second step, their headers projecting the width of a brick plus a mortar joint in front of the step *(below)*. Fill the front and sides, and follow this procedure to the top of the flight. If you are using standard bricks, the bottom riser should be three bricks above ground level and the remaining risers should be three bricks high.

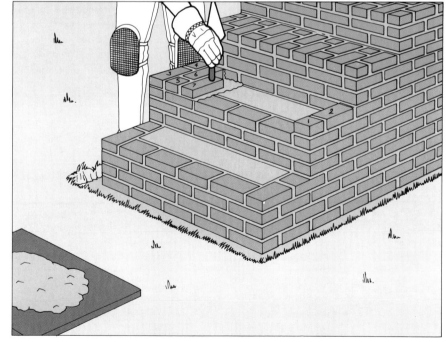

2 **Laying the tread bricks.** Pave the landing, then start laying the tread bricks from the top to avoid mortar stains and having to kneel on newly laid bricks. Lay a half-brick in one corner of the top tread with a full brick behind it; in the opposite corner, lay a full brick with a half-brick behind. Then fill in the middle of the tread, staggering the joints *(above)*. Vary the thickness of the bedding mortar by about 5 mm so that the step slopes downwards for water runoff and check the tread for level crossways. Complete each tread in the same way.

The Many Pattern Possibilities of Tiles

Hard-fired clay tiles, set in mortar over a concrete base, form a paving of exceptional beauty and durability. Usually unglazed, they can be obtained in two varieties suitable for outdoor use—quarry tiles and mosaic tiles.

Quarry tiles are most commonly 150 or 200 mm square, but rectangular and other shapes are also available; for outdoor use, they should be at least 8 mm thick. Some tiles have projecting lugs which make it easier to achieve a uniform joint width between tiles, and anti-slip finishes are recommended for locations which may be exposed to frost. Mosaic tiles are small, between 20 and 75 mm across and between 5 and 10 mm thick; they are usually sold mounted in groups on 300 or 600 mm squares of paper or mesh.

All tiles for outdoor use must be frost-proof, because water absorbed into a tile can freeze and crack it. Only unglazed tiles with a water absorption rate of under 2 per cent—your supplier will know the manufacturer's specifications—can be used safely in cold climates.

To estimate the number of tiles you will need, first calculate the area of the surface to be tiled, then divide it by the size of a tile—remembering to take into account the width of the mortar joints. Add 5 to 10 per cent for wastage.

Ceramic tiles are more durable and require less maintenance when they are set in a mortar made with a latex tile-setting liquid, available from builders' merchants and tile shops. For small jobs use a ready-mixed mortar, adding the latex in place of water and following the manufacturer's instructions. For bigger jobs, make a mortar by mixing 1 part Portland cement to 2 parts fine washed sand and latex according to the manufacturer's instructions.

Mortar joints between ceramic tiles are stronger and more flexible when they are filled with grout that is also mixed with the latex tile-setting liquid instead of water. Ceramic-tile grout comes pre-mixed in a variety of shades in 1.5 to 10 kilogram bags; a 1.5 kilogram bag will fill the joints of about 1 square metre of 200 by 200 mm tiles laid with 6 mm joints. You can also make your own grout by mixing equal proportions of Portland cement and fine washed sand with sufficient latex liquid to make a thick paste.

Before setting the tiles, take time to examine the concrete slab for flaws. Repair cracks, fill holes and smooth out any bumps that are more than 4 mm high, as shown on pages 30–31. Note the position of expansion joints, if any, between sections of slab; try to build your tile pattern around them. For all patterns except those made with tiles of random shapes such as crazy paving *(opposite page, bottom)*, do a dry run of the tile placement. Space the tiles precisely and mark those that need to be cut to fit curving or out-of-square edges. Adjusting the joint between tiles by 1 to 2 mm can sometimes eliminate the need to cut tiles for the edges.

For cutting tiles more than 12 mm thick, you will need an angle grinder or a slab cutter, but tiles less than 12 mm thick are most easily and cheaply cut with a machine cutter *(page 43, above)*. For long shallow curves a tile cutter is ideal, though you can also use tile nippers to chip away curves piece by piece *(page 43, below)*.

When the dry run is complete, pick up the tiles in their order of placement and set them aside. If the layout is very complex, numbering the back of the tiles will help in restoring this sequence. Dampen the slab if the weather is hot and dry, trowel the mortar on, and set the tiles as described on the following pages. Work in small sections; tiles must be laid while the mortar is still soft. If the area is very large, you can break up the job into manageable sections and lay the tiles over several days.

Allow the mortar to cure for a full 24 hours before the joints are grouted, but then do the grouting within the next 24 hours—otherwise the grout may not bond to the mortar. After grouting, allow the surface to dry for 30 minutes, then clean off any grout before it dries on the tiles. To prevent tiles and grout from becoming stained, you can seal the finished paving with a 5 per cent silicone solution. Or you may prefer to use a small brush to seal only the grout, which is usually lighter than the tiles and thus shows stains more readily.

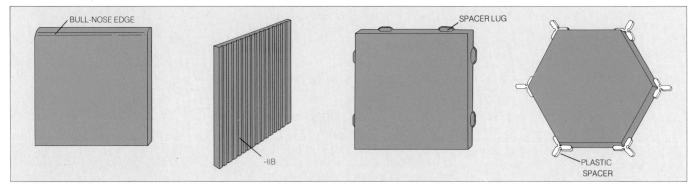

Aids to tile installation. Unglazed quarry tiles are available with a number of features designed to make their installation easier and to accommodate them to special situations. Bull-nose tiles are rounded on either one edge or two—for edges, corners or step caps. Ribbed tiles are scored on the back in parallel ridges to improve the bond between the mortar and tile. Spacer lugs, moulded into the tile edge, ensure that you get even joints between the tiles almost automatically. Serving the same purpose, for tiles that are stamped rather than moulded, are plastic spacer lugs, which are fitted against the corners of each tile as it is laid and are left in place to be covered over later with grout.

Composing Patterns with Shaped Tiles

Repeating a single shape. Paving patterns formed from tiles of a single shape can be remarkably varied. Here, with a section 300 mm square outlined, they range from a simple stacked pattern made by lining up square or rectangular tiles *(below, left)* to the complex honeycomb that practically forms itself when interlocking hexagon or octagon tiles are butted together *(below, centre)*. With mosaic tiles mounted on flexible backing in 300 mm squares, the pattern possibilities are endless, for the tiles are not only varied in shape and colour, but are also available in preassembled modular designs that can be used to form border patterns or all-over repeats of flowers or geometric designs *(below, right)*.

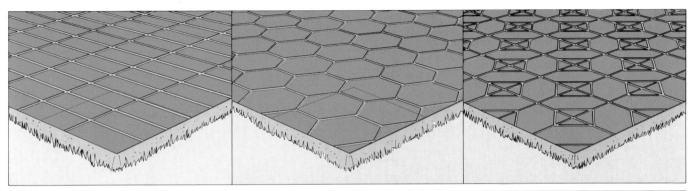

Repeating two shapes. By alternating two tile shapes, you can achieve an intricate pattern that is no more difficult to lay than a single-shape design. The traditional octagon-and-dot pattern *(right, above)* builds automatically with the laying of the first 200 mm octagon, which establishes the placement for all the other octagons and for the intervening squares, or dots. The square-and-picket pattern *(right)*, which mimics a design commonly found in wood parquet floors, builds from a 200 mm square surrounded by four 75 by 280 mm pickets. Together they form the lozenge that becomes the basic unit of the overall tile design.

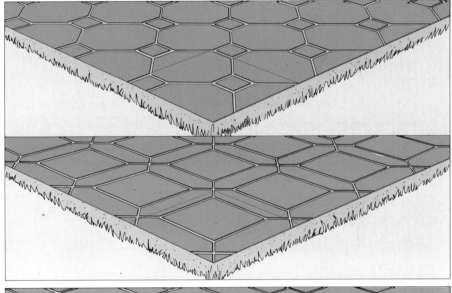

Random patterns from multiple shapes. Square and rectangular slate-coloured tiles in a variety of sizes appear to be set at random to create a mingled pattern *(right, above)* but in fact there is a definite order to the design. Tiles for this kind of pattern are sold in 300 mm squares, although there are a number of ways of placing the tiles within each unit.

Truly random in design is the crazy paving on the right, whose components are simply broken paving tiles with their edges smoothed. These are available by the square metre; designs can be made by outlining sections with a continuous mortar joint.

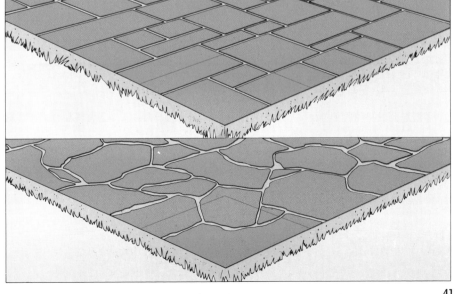

Starting Tile Sequences

Rectangular slabs. For square or rectangular tiles in a simple stack pattern, begin by laying a tile in a corner away from the house, and build outwards from it in an expanding pyramid. If the slab has an expansion joint, set tiles on each side of the joint and establish the apex of the pyramid by laying tiles in the numbered sequence illustrated *(right)*. Work in diagonal rows until the slab is covered; then cut tiles to fill any gaps around the edges.

If the tiles are interlocking hexagons or octagons, start in a corner away from the house by laying a double row of tiles along one side of the slab; then, from the same corner, lay another double row along the other side, following the sequence illustrated *(far right)*. Continue this pattern until the entire slab is covered, bridging expansion joints with tiles. Fill gaps at the edges after you have laid all the full tiles possible.

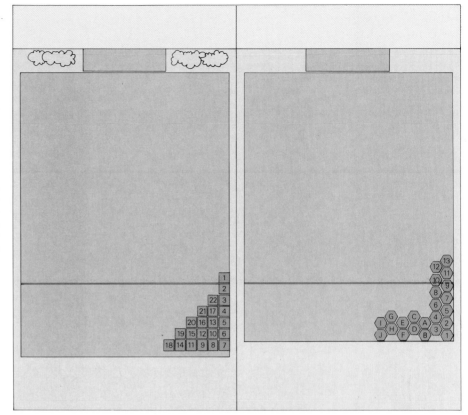

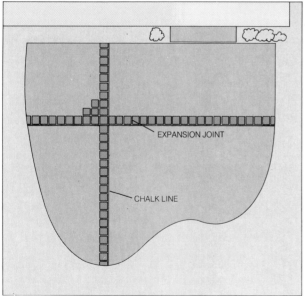

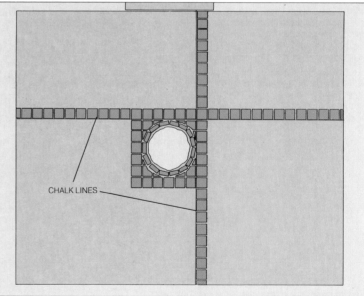

Free-form slabs. If a slab has irregular or curving edges, divide it into quadrants by snapping chalk lines at right angles to each other across its widest dimensions; or use intersecting expansion joints to establish these quadrants. Fill each quadrant with tiles, beginning at the intersecting guidelines and working out to the edges as in the pyramid sequence used in laying the stack pattern *(top, left)*. Trim tiles to fit as necessary.

Interrupted slabs. When appropriate, lay an edging around the obstacle. Snap a chalk line parallel to the front of the house just touching the edging. Snap another chalk line, also tangential to the edging, at right angles to the first. Guided by these lines, build a square around the edging and fill with trimmed tiles. Lay rows of tiles along the chalk quadrant lines and fill each quadrant in the pyramid fashion. Cut the outer tiles in each row to fit the edge of the slab.

Three Techniques
for Cutting Tiles

Using a machine cutter. Set the guide on the cutter to the number of millimetres you want to remove from the tile. Lift the handle bar and place the tile, face up, against the guide. Lower the bar. Holding the tile steady, press down on the movable handle and push it smoothly away from you to score a straight line across the tile.

Place the tile in the clamp at the end of the cutter with the scored line centred under the clamp. Lower the handle bar, then tap it gently with the edge of your open hand. A clean, straight split along the scored line will result.

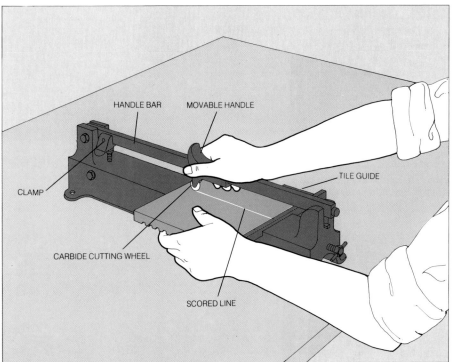

HANDLE BAR   MOVABLE HANDLE

CLAMP

TILE GUIDE

CARBIDE CUTTING WHEEL

SCORED LINE

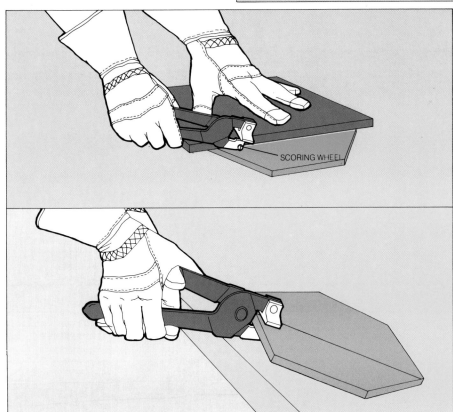

SCORING WHEEL

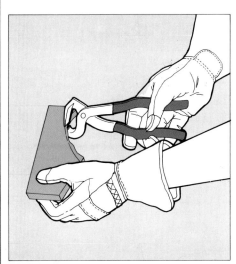

Using a tile cutter. Align a straightedge with the pencil line you have made on the tile to indicate the cut. Run the scoring wheel across the tile in one continuous motion *(above, top)*; press firmly to avoid having to make a second run, which would increase the chance of a ragged break. Grasp the tile between the jaws of the cutter,

aligning the jaws with the centre of the scored line, and squeeze the cutter handles *(above)*. For tiles that are ribbed on the back, the scored line should run at right angles to the ribbing.

To cut a shallow curve with a tile cutter, score a freehand line with the scoring wheel.

Cutting with tile nippers. Grasping the tile firmly in one hand, use the nippers to chip off small pieces of tile. Work in from the edge towards the pencil line indicating the desired shape, and hold the nippers so that the jaws are at an angle to the section of line you are approaching. When the rough cut is complete, smooth the edges with a piece of brick or a small stone.

Laying the Tiles in Mortar

1 Applying the mortar bed. Sweep the area to be tiled to remove all dust and particles. Using the appropriate tile-setting pattern as a guide *(page 42)*, apply a 10 mm-thick layer of mortar over about half a square metre of the area to be tiled first. Use the smooth edge of a rectangular notched trowel to scoop up and spread the mortar; then turn the trowel and draw the notched edge through the mortar, leaving a pattern of uniform ridges. Keep a pointing trowel near for scraping dripped mortar from the slab. Rinse both trowels often in a bucket of water to remove mortar before it dries.

2 Laying the tiles. Following the tile-setting pattern established, set the first tile in the sequence. Hold the tile by its edges and lower it on to the mortar bed, forcing the mortar against the back of the tile. Set plastic spacers against the corners and add a second tile. Continue laying full tiles across the mortar bed, then scrape off the uncovered mortar at the edges with a trowel. Lay a length of timber over the tiles and tap it with a mallet to embed the tiles, checking the surface every four or five tiles for level. Continue until the slab is covered with full tiles; reapply mortar along the edges and add cut tiles as needed.

When you are laying interlocking tiles over an expansion joint, be sure to leave an 8 mm space between the edges of the tiles that lie nearest the joint. Mark the gap with 8 mm spacers *(inset)*.

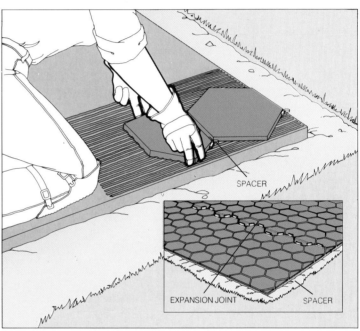

SPACER

EXPANSION JOINT   SPACER

Finishing the Surface

1 Grouting the joints. After allowing the mortar to cure for 24 hours, place small mounds of grout at intervals along the mortar joints over an area of about 1 square metre, and use a dampened wood float or similar tool to spread the grout over the tiles. During this operation, kneel on a piece of plywood to distribute your weight and to avoid displacing the tiles. Moisten the float from time to time by dipping it in a bucket of water.

When grouting an area near an expansion joint, stuff the joint with rolled newspaper to keep it free of grout. This will entail removing the spacers that demarcate the expansion joint.

2 **Cleaning the tiles.** Let the grouted joints dry for 10 minutes, then remove excess grout from the tiles by sweeping a damp sponge across them in a circular motion. Rinse the sponge often in clean water, but keep it barely moist to avoid saturating the grout. Excess water will wash the pigment out of coloured grout.

When all the joints are filled, cover the edge of the slab with a finishing coat of grout, if desired *(page 46)*. Mist the tiled surface every four hours for the first day to let the grout cure slowly. After two more days, remove the lime haze from the tile surface by buffing with a dry cloth.

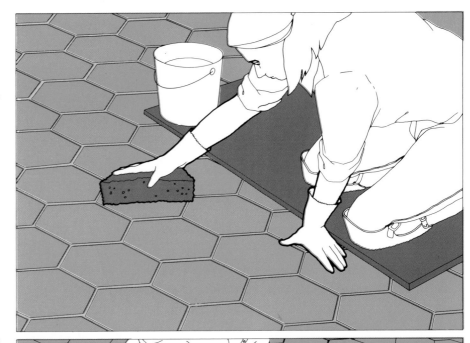

3 **Filling the expansion joint.** After the grout has cured, remove the rolled newspaper from the expansion joint and press lengths of 8 mm caulking strip into the crevice *(right)*. Caulk over the strip with a silicone or polysulphide sealant *(right, below)*, wiping away the excess caulk immediately with the solvent recommended by the manufacturer. Allow the caulk to dry before walking on the tiles.

If you are sealing the tiles, brush two coats of sealer over the tiled surface, or over the joints alone. Be sure that the tilework is completely dry before applying the sealer.

A Finished Edge
for a Tile Slab

Trimming with grout. Using a pointing trowel, apply grout to the exposed edge of the slab. Taper the grout into a wedge shape by holding the trowel at a 45-degree angle to the face of the tiles. Keep the grout damp for the first day of curing by sprinkling it with water every four hours; then allow it to cure an additional three days. Seal as on page 45, Step 3, if desired.

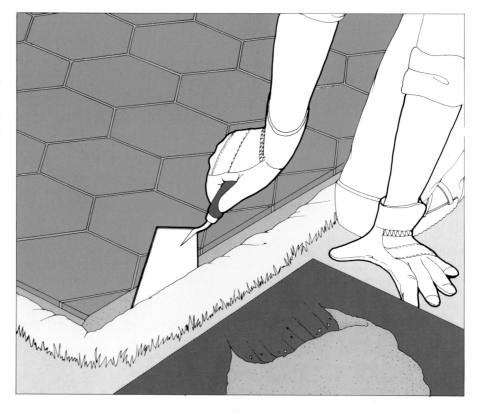

A Tile Veneer
for Concrete Steps

Shaped tiles for a capped step. In laying tiles on concrete steps, first set the risers, then set the treads. Always use a row of whole tiles at the edge of the steps, and cut the second tiles in from the edge, if cutting is necessary. Use bull-nose corner tiles (with two rounded edges) at the corners, and tiles with a single bull-nose edge for rimming the treads and the landing.

When you are planning the tile layout for steps, leave room for a mortar joint between the riser tiles and the tread tiles, one between the riser tiles and the patio floor, and another between the top tread and the house wall.

SINGLE
BULL-NOSE

BULL-NOSE
CORNER

A Flagstone-Paved Patio for a Natural Effect

The rough-hewn appearance and muted colours of flagstone make it an especially attractive surfacing material for patios. Several varieties of stone and slate are used, sliced horizontally into slabs 6 to 30 mm thick. Flagstones can either be lowered into a bed of sand, laid in sand-lime, or set permanently in mortar over a concrete slab. The latter method is recommended for areas where there is a danger of frost, strong wind or heavy rain, and for sloping sites.

Obtaining enough flagstone to cover a large area may take some looking, and buying it may be expensive, but once you have located a source, choose each stone individually. Although part of the charm of flagstone is its irregular shapes and uneven surface, the stones should be of similar thickness to provide a level surface for patio furniture.

When the stones are delivered, have them placed on a tarpaulin next to the slab to prevent their sharp edges from gouging the lawn. Lay out the stones in a dry run; this enables you to rearrange them for the best overall effect and to choose which edges to cut for the best interlocking fit. Let the design dictate the width of the joints, which vary but should be in the range of 10 to 40 mm. Avoid long joint lines, if possible, and leave sizeable gaps between stones to be filled later with the remnants of cut stones.

Most flagstones can be cut with a bolster and club hammer. Some varieties are soft enough to cut to shape with just a few blows of a club hammer, while others are so hard that they need to be scored first with a silicon carbide masonry blade fitted to an angle grinder before a bolster will break them cleanly.

After the dry run is complete, you will need to devise a system for keeping the stones in order as you lift them to prepare the mortar bed. The simplest solution is to lift them a section at a time, arranging them beside the slab in the same pattern they formed on the slab.

Because flagstones are heavy and the joints wide, both mortar and grout should be weaker and thicker than the consistency used for tiles. The actual mixture varies according to the density of the stone. For a heavy granite, cement and builders' sand are mixed in proportions of 1 to 2 or 3; while for a lighter sandstone, the proportions are 1 to 7 or 8. If there is any movement in the concrete base, it is preferable that cracks should develop in the mortar rather than the stone.

Flagstones, like tiles, should be cleaned immediately after grouting, within 10 minutes. When the mortar and grout have cured, you may seal the joints with a masonry sealant.

Veneering a Concrete Slab with Flagstones

1 Marking stones for cutting. Arrange the flagstones over the concrete slab in a suitable pattern. Wherever a stone overlaps the edge of the slab, mark it with a pencil line, using the edge of the slab as a guide. Where one of the stones overlaps another, mark adjacent stones with interlocking cutting lines, allowing for a 10 to 40 mm joint between them. You may lay stones directly over expansion joints, if there are any. Leave all of the marked stones in position until the entire slab has been covered.

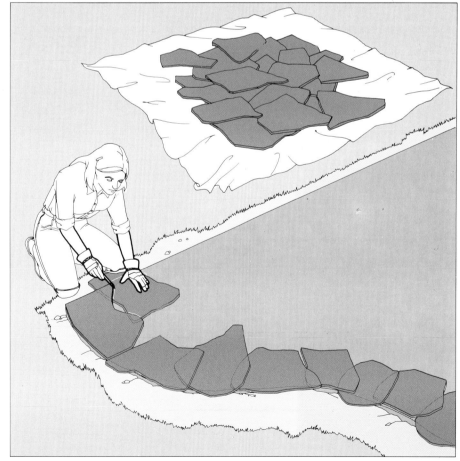

2 **Cutting the stones.** Remove the marked stones one by one and score them with a bolster and club hammer. Hold the bolster against the pencil line and tap it several times with the club hammer *(right);* then move the bolster along the line and tap again. Continue until a breaking line has been scored across the stone. If the stone is more than 25 mm thick, score a second line on the reverse side of the stone, directly over the first. To establish this second line, extend the first line down the edges of the stone and trace a connecting line on the back.

Rest the stone on a length of timber, the scored line overhanging the edge of the timber. Then tap the overhanging portion with the club hammer until the piece snaps off *(far right).* As each stone is cut, return it to its position on the slab.

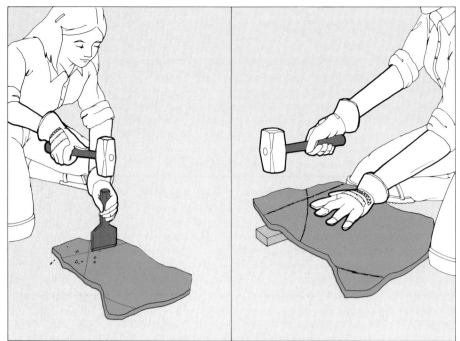

3 **Seating and levelling the stones.** Remove a section of stones, beginning at a corner or along an edge, and trowel on a 25 mm-thick mortar bed with a notched trowel as shown on page 44. Then replace the stones and seat them in the mortar by laying a length of timber on the stones and tapping along its length with a club hammer. Check to make sure that the stones are level; if a stone sits higher than the rest, scoop out some of the mortar from beneath it with a pointing trowel. If it sits too low, lift the flagstone and trowel additional mortar into the cavity.

After you have laid all the flagstones, allow at least 48 hours before walking on the patio or attempting to grout the gaps.

4 **Grouting the joints.** Apply grout along the joints with a pointing trowel. Then use the tip of a concave jointer to push the grout into the joints to a depth 2 mm below the stone surface. Clean off any excess grout that clings to the stones. Mist the stonework with water every four hours for the first day, and let the grout cure three days before walking on the patio.

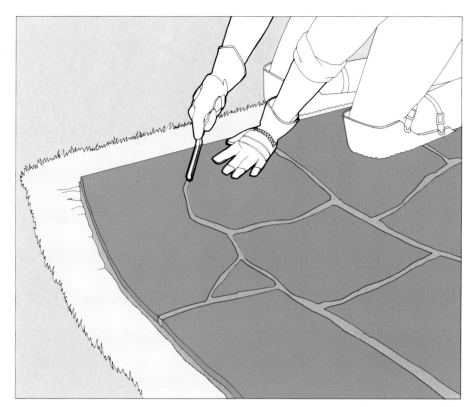

Laying Flagstone Steps

Veneering a stepped slab with stone. When cutting flagstones to fit step risers, leave space above and below the stones for mortar joints. Cut stone treads to overhang the risers by 25 mm. Plot the layout and set the stones in mortar as for a slab *(pages 47–48, Steps 1–3),* but during the laying process, wedge a length of 50 by 25 mm softwood against the underside of the tread to provide a temporary support for the grout in the overhanging section of the tread. After the grout has cured for three days, remove the support.

2 Increasing the Comfort Quotient

All-weather protection. A canvas awning fixed over an outdoor patio will provide shelter from both showers of rain and the glare of the summer sun. The canvas is lashed to eyebolts that have been screwed into sturdy timber beams. Synthetic rope used to secure the awning can be easily untied, allowing the covering to be removed for storage during the winter months.

"Everybody talks about the weather," observed Mark Twain, "but nobody does anything about it." Happily for owners of outdoor patios, this is not entirely true. Although no one has succeeded in altering major weather patterns, people have always created an agreeable microclimate for themselves—witness the fire at the mouth of the cave.

In adapting a patio to the vagaries of the weather, you will be dealing largely with the characteristic patterns of temperature, humidity, rainfall and wind for your locality—patterns for which the local weather station can supply a profile. But you may also be dealing with weather conditions specific to your site, which must be observed firsthand. If your house is on a hilltop, a patio may be buffeted by strong winds. In built-up areas, nearby structures may create wind funnels or unusual cycles of sun and shade across your patio.

Once, when houses had the luxury of many outdoor living spaces—verandas, patios, gazebos—people escaped from sharp winds, hot sun or a swarm of flies by moving from one place to another. Nowadays, with limited space, baffles and screens provide the same results. Louvres or woven blinds secured to a simple wooden framework will shelter a patio from the glare of the midday sun; a canvas awning will keep off showers of rain; rafters and crosspieces provide pathways for climbing plants and vines. And around the sides of a patio, a phalanx of windbreaks will tame blustery breezes.

On a suitably reinforced concrete patio, a completely enclosed structure will provide more substantial shelter. A glass-walled conservatory need be neither so grand nor so expensive as the word suggests, and the "greenhouse effect" produced by its glazed walls and roof will allow the patio to be used throughout the year. A sliding glass door installed in the house or conservatory wall will not only invite your family and friends to step outdoors but will unite indoors with out, making one an extension of the other.

With weather-related troubles under control, you can address yourself to making your new living space enjoyable in other ways. One desirable improvement, especially in high-density neighbourhoods, is increased privacy. The overhead screen or freestanding fence that dims the sun or curbs the wind will in addition work to intercept the gaze of passers-by and neighbours.

As a final touch, you will want to add furnishings appropriate to your family's outdoor activities—built-in benches to seat a crowd, a comfortable canvas sling chair for reading, a picnic table for alfresco dining. That done, your new patio will get maximum use—more than justifying the labour of creating it.

Coverings That Modulate the Sun's Rays

A simple overhead covering will both shelter an open patio from glaring sunlight and help to integrate it with the architecture of the house. Coverings may be either temporary or permanent, and can be constructed from a variety of materials.

The post-and-beam structural support for the covering must be planned with care and built with timber specially treated to resist decay. Generally, 75 by 75 mm timber is acceptable for the corner posts, which are anchored to the patio with post shoes. Rafters, the two front beams and the ledger should all be 50 mm thick. To calculate the correct depth for these, divide the distance they will span (measured in millimetres) by 20, add 20 to the result, and then choose the nearest standard-size timber to this figure. Thus, a 3 metre span as shown on the right requires a ledger 175 mm deep (3000 mm divided by 20 equals 150; plus 20 equals 170). Decorative ends on the beams and rafters should be cut before actual construction work begins. If you wish to pitch the roof to shed rainwater off a solid covering, draw a scale plan of the structure to determine the angle at which the rafters slope. A difference in height of more than 75 mm between the front beams and the ledger will be sufficient. The inner ends of the rafters must be cut to the required angle before they are installed. The outer ends may be either notched to fit square on top of the front beams, or slotted into notches cut into the beams; alternatively the beams can be bevelled to the slope of the rafters.

The simplest form of shade for an open patio is a patterned grid of crosspieces nailed between rafters *(page 56)*. Providing light shade, it is especially useful for an open patio that receives sun for only part of the day. The grid can serve as the basis for a denser covering of timber slats, spaced at whatever intervals and in whatever configuration you choose *(page 57, above)*. Alternatively it can provide support for climbing plants *(below)*.

A permanent form of roofing for the post-and-beam structure that regulates the amount of sunlight reaching the patio and requires little maintenance consists of slanted louvres secured between the rafters *(page 55)*. The angle at which you set the louvres will depend on the latitude at which you live; in most areas, an angle of 40 to 50 degrees will give sufficient protection, but a lower angle, about 30 degrees, may be necessary for hotter climates. By choosing the direction in which the louvres are slanted, you can admit sunlight in the morning and provide shade in the afternoon, or reverse the effect.

Panels of woven reed slotted between rafters *(pages 55–56)* can be removed and stored elsewhere when not in use. The material has a short life expectancy, but it is cheap and easy to replace. Available at garden centres, it is sold in rolls of varying lengths and widths, and can be trimmed to size with metal shears.

Also suitable for temporary installation during the summer only is a canvas awning *(page 57, below)*. For maximum durability, choose a synthetic canvas—either acrylic or vinyl-coated polyester. Both are treated to resist rot, fire, fading and water, and can be expected to last five to eight years if stored in a dry place over the winter. To increase the awning's life, hose it down at least twice a year and scrub it with a long-handled brush to remove dirt and leaves which cause rot. Ensure the fabric is dry before storing it; though treated to resist mildew, it is not mildew-proof.

A manufacturer will supply the awning to your own specifications. Make sure that it is cut 100 mm smaller all round than your frame so that you can tie it in place. The edges should be reinforced, with one eyelet in each corner, two eyelets 75 mm from each corner and the remainder spaced at intervals of no more than 300 mm.

The Versatile Climber: a Living Sun Screen

When it comes to providing protection from the sun for a patio, nature supplies what is perhaps the most accommodating sun screen of all. Unlike fixed louvres, which never vary in their function, or a canvas canopy, which must be taken down if you want more sun, climbers are endlessly adaptable. Chosen and placed with care, a climber trained over a trellis *(page 56, below)* will control not only how much shade you get but when you get it.

A climbing plant can be annual or perennial, evergreen or deciduous. With a morning glory or a cup-and-saucer vine, both of which can grow as much as 8 metres in their single season of life, you can have, in effect, instant cover. Wisteria and fox grape will cool a patio in summer and then, in the autumn, drop their leaves to let the welcome winter sun enter the house.

The density of shade will depend partly on the climber's habit of growth, partly on the size and translucency of its leaves. Climbers fall into three categories. Some cling by means of hooks, thorns or tendrils; others twine around supports; and some, such as roses and jasmines, are leaners that droop unless supported.

Twiners tend to provide the deepest shade. Similarly, the large, coarse leaves of the hop vine, which can measure as much as 200 mm across, overlap one another to create a curtain that can virtually blot out the sun, as can the leathery leaves of English ivy; while the delicate, deeply cut leaves of the balloon vine simply filter the sunshine.

In addition to providing cover, many climbers have decorative flowers and fruits—but these can be a mixed blessing. Remember when you are choosing your living sun screen that grapes attract bees and that birds will come to feed on the berries of bittersweet—and litter the patio floor. Also, some intriguing flowers, such as those of the Dutchman's pipe, have an objectionable smell.

Building a Durable Framework

1 **Attaching the ledger.** Mark the planned height of the ledger on the house wall directly above the sides of the patio. Snap a level chalk line between the two points, and drive a masonry nail part way into the wall at each end of the marked line. Cut a ledger from 175 by 50 mm timber to the exact length of the patio, then drill 9 mm holes through it at 300 mm intervals. With a helper, raise the ledger and rest it on the masonry nails; mark the fixing positions on the house wall, then lower the ledger. Drill 15 mm-diameter holes 100 mm into the wall at the marked positions. Secure the ledger to the wall with 100 mm expanding anchors; slip all the anchors into position and tighten each one with a spanner.

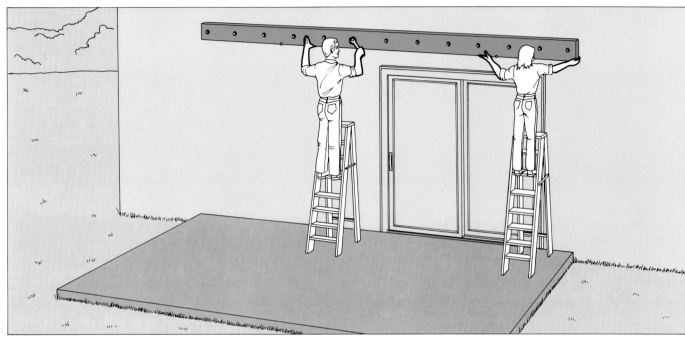

2 **Erecting the posts.** Position a post shoe at one corner of the patio, with its base plate about 50 mm in from the front and side edges. Mark the positions of the fixing holes, then drill a hole of the appropriate diameter and about 75 mm deep at each mark. Secure the post shoe to the patio with expanding anchors. Cut two posts long enough to reach from the shoe to a point level with the bottom of the rafter. With a helper, slot one of the posts into the shoe, screwing or bolting it in place as appropriate. Install the opposite post in the same way.

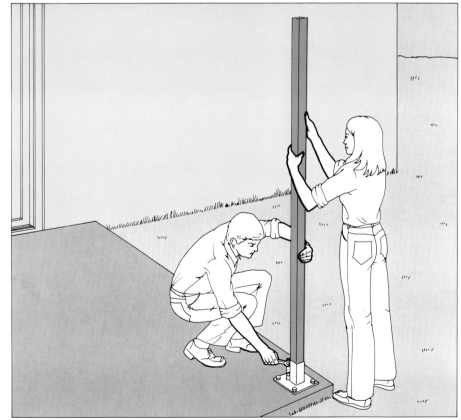

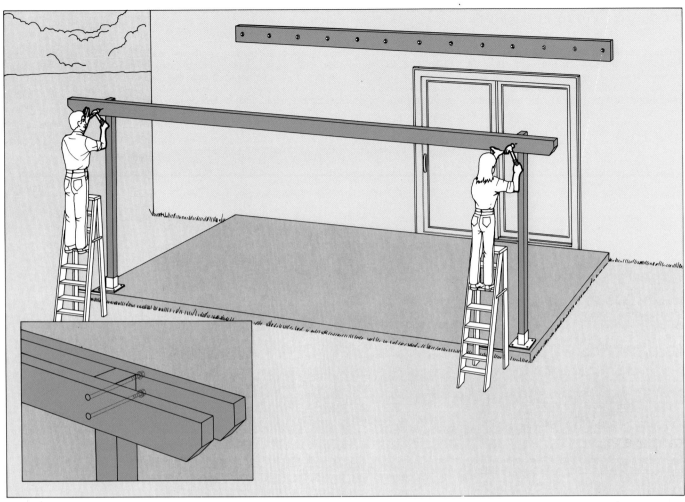

3 **Mounting the beams.** Cut two 175 by 50 mm beams 600 mm longer than the patio. With a helper, hold one beam against the outside of the posts so that its upper edge is flush with the tops of the posts and there is an equal overhang at each side; then check for level and fix it temporarily to each post with a 75 mm round-wire nail. Attach the second beam to the inside of the posts. Using a long 12 mm bit, drill two holes—one above the other—through each post-and-beam as-sembly, and secure the assembly with long 12 mm coach bolts and washers *(inset)*. Cut spacers 75 mm wide by 100 mm long and as deep as the beams (175 mm here) and nail them between the beams at about 300 mm intervals.

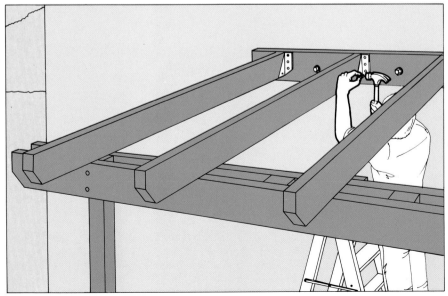

4 **Fitting the rafters.** Mark the face of the ledger for rafters at intervals of about 400 mm, making sure that the outside edge of each end rafter will be flush with the outside face of a post. Centre and nail a 150 mm metal joist hanger over each pair of lines, then mark identically spaced lines on top of the beams. Cut the rafters about 200 mm longer than the width of the patio and lift the first one into position. At the house end, fit the rafter into a joist hanger and nail it in place. At the beam end, toenail the rafter into both sides of the beam, using two 75 mm round-wire nails on each side. Attach the remaining rafters in the same way.

A Louvred Sun Screen

Assembling the louvres. With a protractor and a sliding bevel, mark a length of 100 by 25 mm timber with a series of parallel lines angled at 50 degrees, spacing the lines 100 mm apart. Cut along the lines with a circular saw, then nail the first pair of spacers to the beam ends of two facing rafters. In the example shown, it is assumed that the patio is on the east side of the house and that the intention is to provide morning sunlight and afternoon shade. This is achieved by aligning the lower edges of the spacers with the lower edges of the rafters and slanting the spacers down towards the house. The inner edges of the spacers should be flush with the inner edge of the second beam.

Cut a 150 by 25 mm louvre to fit between the two rafters and nail it to the first pair of spacers. Nail a second pair of spacers to the rafters *(right)* and attach a second louvre. Repeat this process until the entire row has been filled. Cut a pair of spacers to fit between the last louvre and the ledger, then nail them into place. Fit louvres and spacers between all the other rafters in the same way *(inset)*.

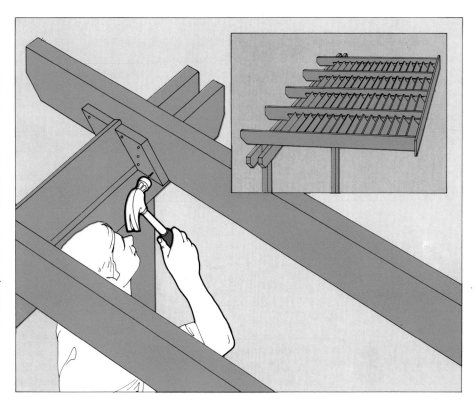

A Removable Covering of Woven Reed

1 **Fixing support cleats.** To support panels of woven reed, nail 50 by 25 mm cleats along the inner faces of each rafter, lining up the lower edge of the cleat with the lower edge of the rafter. The cleats should extend from the inner edge of the second front beam to the joist hangers.

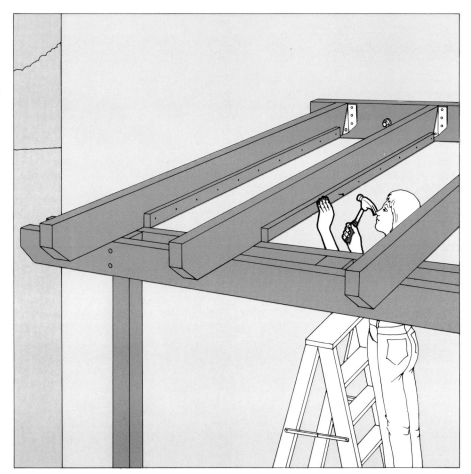

2 **Making the panels.** Using four pieces of 50 by 50 mm timber, make up a frame to fit between the rafters: glue and nail the shorter end pieces across the ends of the longer side pieces. Place woven-reed fencing over one of the frames, and fasten it to the edges of the frame with heavy-duty staples spaced 50 to 75 mm apart *(right)*. Trim off any excess with metal shears. Cover all the frames in the same fashion, then lower them into place, allowing them to rest loosely on the cleats *(inset)*.

Coverings for Different Degrees of Shade

A trellis for light shade. Mark the positions for the crosspieces along the lower edges of the two outer rafters. Snap a chalk line between each pair of marks on the two sides to transfer the measurements to the intervening rafters. With a combination square, transfer these marks to the vertical faces of each rafter, then cut crosspieces to fit between the rafters where marked and above the spacers between the beams. Nail each crosspiece to its rafters, butt-nailing one end and toe-nailing the other, with 75 mm galvanized lost-head nails punched in below the surface.

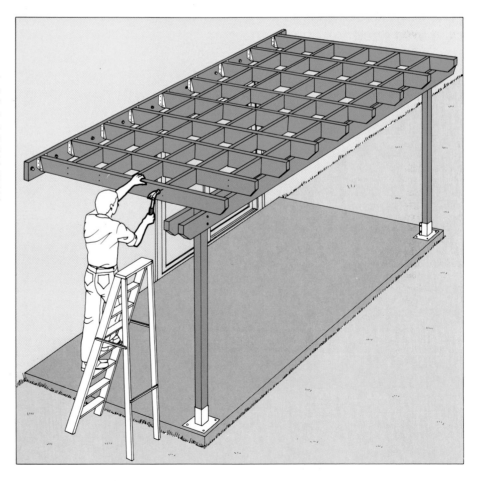

A chequerboard grid for deeper shade. Using the trellis *(opposite page, below)* as a base, top each square with lengths of 50 by 50 mm timber. Start off with a corner square at one end of the ledger, placing the first slat across two rafters, its ends at the midpoint of the edge of the rafters. Centre the second slat between the rafters at the opposite side of the square, aligning its outer edge with the midpoint of the crosspiece *(right)*. Fill the rest of the square with more 50 by 50 mm slats, spaced at equal intervals. Secure the slats to the rafters using two 75 mm nails at each end of each slat.

On an adjacent square, reverse the direction of the slats so that they run across two crosspieces. Continue in this fashion, changing the direction of the slats on adjacent squares to create a chequerboard pattern *(inset)*.

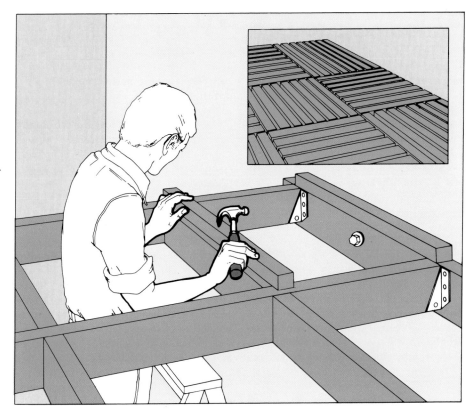

A Canvas Awning for Deep Shade

Attaching the cover. Two outer rafters and a board of the same depth as the rafters nailed above the front beams provide framing supports for the covering at the sides and front.

To tie a canvas awning in place, screw in 75 mm eyebolts along the ledger, outer rafters and front board, spacing them to line up with the eyelets stitched into the awning. Using synthetic cord tied with double reef knots, first secure the two corner eyelets at either end of the wall side of the awning to their eyebolts. Take another length of cord, tie one end to a corner eyebolt and thread the free end through the adjoining eyelet; continue lacing eyebolts and eyelets until you reach the end of the wall side. Lace the opposite corners and side in the same way. With a helper, tighten the lacing on both sides; keep the canvas centred between the front board and the ledger. Repeat this procedure for the two remaining sides.

Windbreaks to Deflect Wind and Prying Eyes

In their primary role, windbreaks serve to moderate strong or annoying winds and turn them into welcome breezes. But the windbreaks shown on these pages can serve a secondary purpose as well. Their post-and-rail framework can be filled in with wood or canvas for privacy or fitted with transparent panels of plastic to preserve a spectacular view.

In planning a windbreak you will first need to determine its orientation. Your weather centre can tell you the direction of the prevailing wind in your area; but this can be affected by the season of the year and features of topography such as hills, valleys and bodies of water.

The shape of the frame you build for the windbreak can be straight or curved. A curved windbreak will deflect wind somewhat more effectively than a straight one (below), although it may limit your choice of coverings. But in most cases the covering itself will have an even greater effect on wind flow. In general, a partly open or louvred covering reduces wind pressure by

diffusing it; a solid barrier concentrates it, generating strong down-draughts on the opposite side of the windbreak, directly on to the patio or deck.

The height and width of the windbreak determine how large an area is protected. For example, a solid windbreak completely changes the pattern of an air current for a distance equal to one and a half times its height and alters the current to some extent over a distance equal to 10 to 15 times its height.

Check your local building regulations before planning to carry the height of a windbreak to more than 2 metres—the usual limit on any kind of fencing. If you must protect a very large area, your only legal alternative may be to plant a natural windbreak of trees, such as a row of conifers, which will eventually grow to an effective height and density.

In most localities the posts for a windbreak may be anchored directly in the soil. Allow for a hole from a third to a half the above-ground height of the post; for ex-

ample, you will need an 800 to 1200 mm hole for a windbreak 2.4 metres high. But if you live in an area with extremely high winds or loose soil—such as sand or built-up earth—you will need to anchor the posts with concrete footings. Dig the holes for the footings 450 mm wide, and lay a 100 mm layer of gravel at the bottom of each hole. Then set the posts and fill the hole to the top with concrete, sloping the top of the concrete up the post so that it will shed water. All posts should be pressure-treated to retard decay.

Wood is the most versatile covering material for a windbreak frame, adapting to many designs; although not as cheap as canvas, it is reasonably inexpensive. Select timber with a straight grain and as few unsightly knots as possible. If you wish to preserve a stunning view beyond the windbreak, you can use transparent acrylic; the disadvantages are that it scratches easily and may eventually discolour. Acrylic sheets are available in various sizes up to 2400 by 1200 mm.

A Choice of Windbreak Shapes

Straight and curved frames. A windbreak with a straight frame, consisting of 100 by 50 mm rails set in fence-rail brackets between 100 by 100 mm posts, offers the greatest choice of covering materials and patterns (page 60), but its flat shape meets the force of the wind head-on and tends to deflect it upwards, over the top of the barrier (inset). The more decorative curved frame, built of 150 by 25 mm reinforced rails bent around 100 by 100 mm posts, can be covered only with vertical slats or boards. But it is structurally stronger and resists violent gusts better, because it diverts some air sideways, around the outside of the crescent.

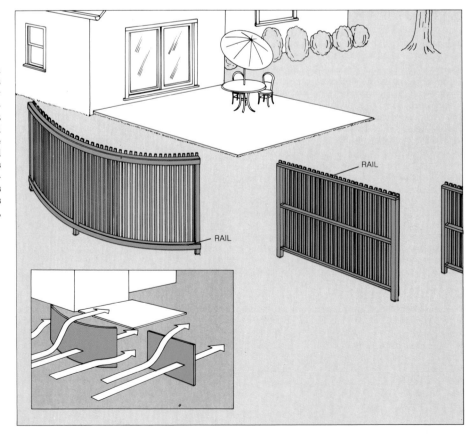

Building a Basic Screen with Vertical Slats

1 Setting the frame posts. Stretch a string between two stakes to indicate the location of the windbreak, and dig post holes at 1.8 metre intervals along the string. Set the 100 by 100 mm posts in the holes, aligning them with the string. Then, while you plumb each post with a level, ask a helper to nail two 50 by 25 mm braces to each post, setting each pair to form a right angle and anchoring them against stakes angled to hold the braces steady. Then fill each post hole with soil, compacting it around the post by tamping it with the end of a 100 by 50 mm board.

To level the tops of the posts, first stretch a string between the end posts at a height 6 mm below the top of the lowest post in the row *(inset)*, using as your guide a line level or spirit level placed at the centre of the taut string. Mark the posts at the string line, then use a steel square to extend the mark around each post. Cut off the tops of the posts with a circular saw.

Measure between the outside edges of the end posts, and cut a 100 by 50 mm cap rail to this length. Nail the rail across the tops of the posts, covering the exposed end-grain to forestall rot.

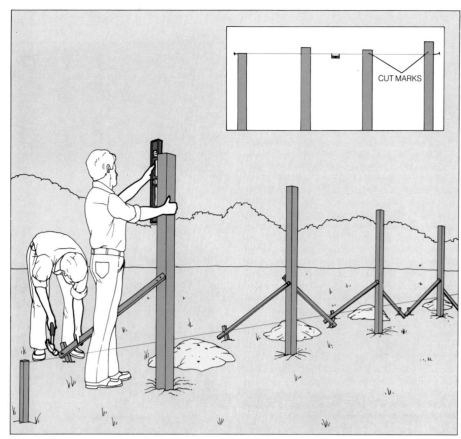

CUT MARKS

FENCE-RAIL BRACKET

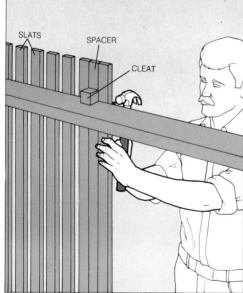

SLATS SPACER CLEAT

2 Fitting the rails. Mark the position for 100 by 50 mm bottom rails with a stretched string and a line level, as you did in establishing the tops of the posts *(Step 1)*. Set the string roughly 200 mm above the ground. Mount metal fence-rail brackets or angle brackets on all of the posts at this height. To fit a rail between two posts, hold it against the posts at the marks, place a ruler against the inside edge of the posts

and scribe the rail along the rule. Cut off the rail just inside the scribed lines, slip it into the brackets, and then nail it in place.

For windbreaks needing a centre rail, such as the plywood panels and diagonal boards on page 60, stretch a horizontal string half way between the cap rail and the bottom rail. Install each section of centre rail in the same way.

3 Installing standard slats. Cut 50 by 25 mm slats to the desired height; they usually begin 100 mm above the ground and extend 100 mm above the top rail. Plumb the first slat, and nail it on to the rails. Then install the remaining slats, using a piece of scrap wood as a spacer. Tack a wooden cleat to the spacer so that it hangs from the cap rail at the height of the first slat. Use the spacer to align the top ends of the slats and to space the slats equidistant from each other.

Optional Designs for Windbreak Coverings

A covering for every purpose. The windbreaks shown here represent a range of compromises among wind control, privacy and landscape design, some favouring one quality over the others. Lattice panels, screwed to the posts, are most effective in diffusing wind and offer some privacy. A louvred windbreak of vertical or horizontal 150 by 25 mm boards directs the wind up, down or sideways and blocks one angle of view completely; the ends of the louvres are nailed into an inner frame of 100 by 25 mm boards which is then set into the supporting frame. Windbreaks covered in the board-and-board style or with painted plywood or chipboard panels, both of which diffuse the wind, are easy to build; the boards are simply nailed to both sides of the frame vertically or horizontally. In one variation of the design, the boards are set diagonally over sections of the frame.

For a bright backdrop, coloured canvas sheets, positioned to allow air to pass around the edges, may be lashed to the frame with cotton rope that passes between eyelets in the canvas and screw eyes set into the frame. A windbreak fitted with panels of clear acrylic, held in place on all four sides by a double frame of 50 by 25 mm stops and a bead of silicone sealant, saves a pleasant vista—but its solid shape may cause downdraughts over the patio. The wooden basketweave pattern, available as a unit ready to install, is screwed to the posts; it ensures privacy and directs air down on to the patio.

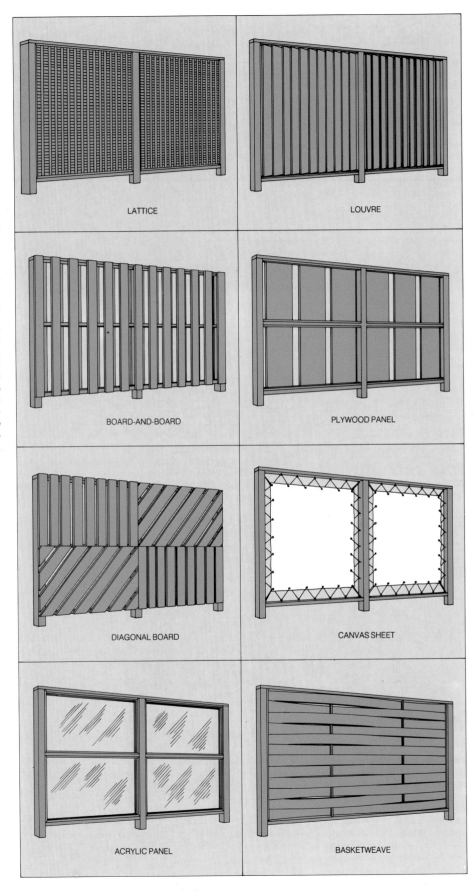

LATTICE

LOUVRE

BOARD-AND-BOARD

PLYWOOD PANEL

DIAGONAL BOARD

CANVAS SHEET

ACRYLIC PANEL

BASKETWEAVE

Building a Curved Windbreak

1 **Laying out the crescent.** Drive in two 50 by 25 mm stakes, about 450 mm long, 150 mm to each side of the centre of the windbreak location. Bend a 150 by 25 mm rail at least 4.5 metres long around them into the desired arc; brace it with a temporary stake 450 mm in from each end. If the rail is not flexible enough, cut 15 mm kerfs every 75 mm *(inset)*, using a circular saw. Set 100 by 100 mm posts *(page 59, Step 1)* every 1.8 metres along the outside of the curve.

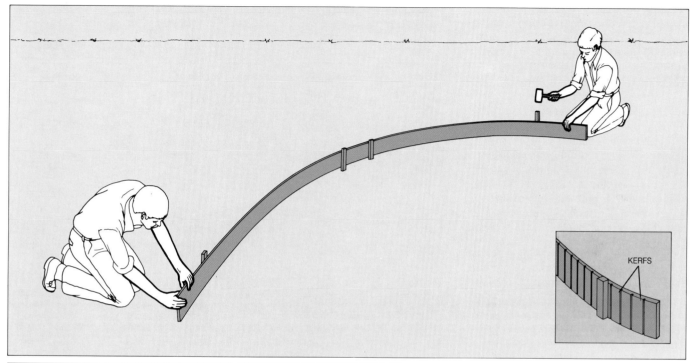

KERFS

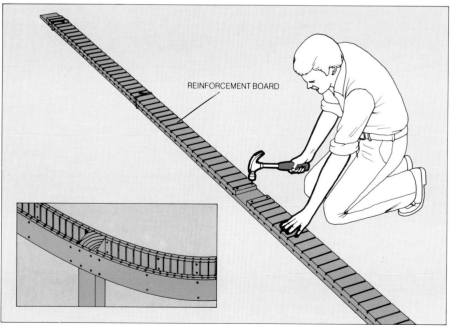

REINFORCEMENT BOARD

2 **Making reinforcement boards.** Temporarily tack a 150 by 25 mm upper rail to the posts, and mark the post locations on the back of the rail; this rail should be long enough to span the entire windbreak. Remove the rail, measure between the marks to determine the exact distance between posts, and cut 150 by 25 mm reinforcement boards to these lengths. Kerf these shorter boards *(Step 1, inset)* so that they bend to the curve of the rail.

3 **Reinforcing the rail.** Tie and tack the reinforcement boards loosely to the back of the upper rail between the marks made in Step 2, and then nail the rail permanently to the posts and to the reinforcement boards. Add a second rail, with reinforcement boards, to the other side of the posts in the same way *(inset)*. Then reinforce and install pairs of bottom rails to complete the frame. Cut and install vertical slats following the instructions on page 59, Step 3.

Outdoor Furniture: Invitation to Relax

No porch, deck or patio is complete without a place to sit and a table for alfresco dining. The benches, seats and tables on the following pages are sturdy—an essential quality for any outdoor structure. Because you build them yourself—a task that takes no more than a weekend—they can be tailored to suit your own particular needs.

The picnic table shown on the right is a classic item of outdoor furniture, but there are any number of design possibilities. Backless benches, made of 50 by 25 mm slats supported by 100 by 100 mm pedestals, can be made any length and can be curved to follow the contours of a free-form patio *(page 64)*. If you plan to cover the slab with a veneer of bricks, tiles or stones, anchor the pedestals first so that you can veneer around them.

Wooden furniture meant for outdoor use may vary considerably in design, but the choice of suitable materials is limited. Only a few woods are sufficiently resistant to decay and insects to be used outdoors. Pressure-treated pine is the least expensive but has a tendency to warp. Cedar and redwood stand up well and can be painted, stained or sealed; even untreated, they resist the elements, and they weather to an attractive grey. For fasteners, the choice is between rustproof galvanized-steel screws or ring-shanked or twisted nails.

Wood is not always the most practical material, however. In a damp climate, furniture made of rigid PVC (plastic) pipe provides a handsome alternative. It is lightweight, movable and completely weatherproof. Fitted with canvas slings and waterproof cushions—which you can make from plasticized fabric and foam or purchase from a garden furniture supplier—it is also extremely comfortable.

The pipes and fittings are available at plumbing shops and large D.I.Y. stores. PVC furniture can be painted with acrylic paint once it is built or it can be left as is—it comes in white, grey and black.

A One-Piece Picnic Table

Anatomy of a picnic table. This traditional 1200 by 925 mm trestle table with integral benches is made of 100 by 50 mm and 150 by 37 mm boards. The 150 by 37 mm boards forming the tabletop are held together by three 100 by 50 mm cleats. Fastened to the end cleats are two pairs of 100 by 50 mm legs, crossed by two 100 by 50 mm arms that support the 150 by 37 mm boards of the seats. For added stability, 100 by 50 mm braces run from the centre cleat to the bench arms. The structure is fastened with galvanized bolts, wood screws and nails.

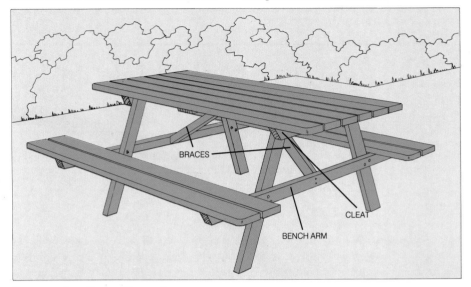

Putting the Parts Together

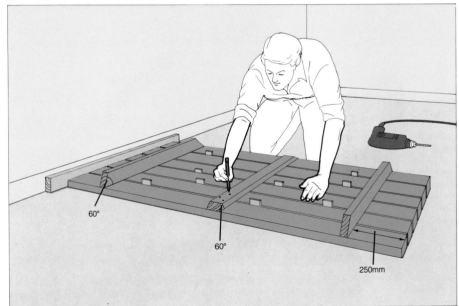

1 **Assembling the tabletop.** On a flat surface, lay out six 150 by 37 mm boards, 2 metres long, bracing their ends against a straight, rigid support. Set 5 mm spacers between the boards. Cut three 100 by 50 mm cleats 925 mm long, mitring the ends at opposite 60-degree angles; mitre two of the cleats on edge and set them 250 mm in from the ends of the tabletop; mitre the third cleat flat and set it across the centre.

Mark screw positions—two for each board—in a zigzag pattern on the middle cleat, in a straight line on each end cleat.

Fasten the cleats to the top, drilling pilot holes for 63 mm screws at the marks. On the end cleats, drill a 50 mm countersunk hole in one edge and a pilot hole in the other; to match the holes, draw a squared guideline around the cleat and bisect the line on each edge.

2 Joining the legs and bench arms. Cut two bench arms 1600 mm long, and four legs 800 mm long, from 100 by 50 mm timber. Mitre the ends of the bench arms at opposite 60-degree angles, and the ends of the legs at parallel 75-degree angles. Measure along the longer edge of each bench arm 350 mm in from both ends, and mark a 75-degree angle slanted in the opposite direction from the nearest mitred end. Tack the table legs to the bench arms just inside these marks, positioning each leg so that its outside edge extends 350 mm below the bench arm. Drill two 10 mm holes, diagonal to each other, through each leg and the bench arm. Insert a 90 mm coach bolt through each hole, bolt head on the bench-arm side, and fasten the legs to the bench arms.

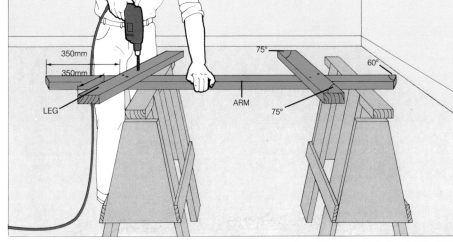

3 Fastening the legs to the cleats. Clamp the top of a leg assembly to the inside of an end cleat so that the legs are equal distances from the edges of the tabletop, and drill two 10 mm holes, diagonally spaced, through the cleat and each leg. Fasten the legs to the cleats with 90 mm coach bolts, bolt heads on the cleat side.

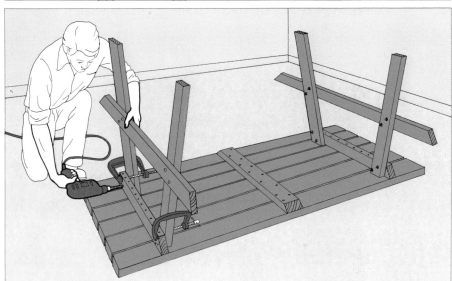

4 Installing the diagonal braces. Cut two 100 by 50 mm boards 840 mm long. Using a sliding bevel set at 120 degrees, mark parallel lines to form angles at both ends of each board. At one end of each board, measure in 35 mm from the apex of the 120-degree angle along the slanted line; from there extend a second line, at right angles to the first, to the edge of the board (*inset*). Cut the boards along the marked lines. Butt the double-cut end of each brace against the midpoint of the centre cleat; butt the other end of each brace against a bench arm. Using 75 mm oval nails, toenail the sides of the braces into the centre cleat and the tabletop. Then nail through the bench arms into the ends of the braces (*right*).

Add seats by laying two 150 by 37 mm boards across the bench-arm extensions, spacing the boards 5 mm apart. Drive oval nails through the boards into the bench arms.

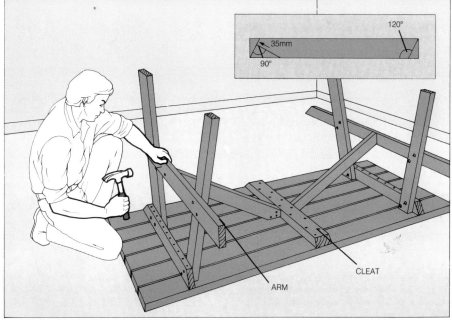

Bending a Bench Along a Curved Patio

1 Establishing post positions. Mark off chalk lines around the edge of the patio at 900 mm intervals, beginning approximately 150 mm from the planned end of the bench. To measure these intervals, use a strip of 3 mm hardboard, 900 mm long and 50 mm wide, bent to follow the curve of the patio edge.

Cut a 100 by 100 mm post, 690 mm high, for each post position. Then notch the top of each post on two opposing faces, cutting the notches 100 mm long and 30 mm deep.

2 Installing the posts. Anchor the posts 300 mm deep in concrete footings *(page 58)*, leaving 390 mm above ground; then attach two 100 by 50 mm cross-braces to the top of each post. Make the braces 450 mm long, and centre them in the notches. Tack them in place temporarily while you drill two 10 mm holes, diagonally spaced, through the braces and posts. Fasten the braces with 125 mm coach bolts.

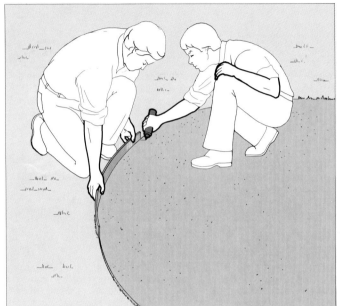

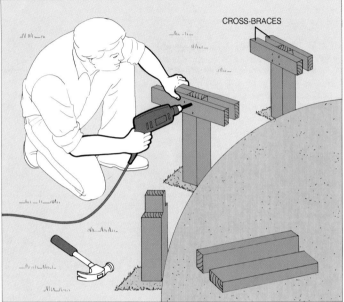

3 Attaching the slats. Nail rows of 50 by 25 mm slats, edge up, across the top of the cross-braces, beginning on the inside curve of the bench and at the midpoint of the curve. Position the first slat so that it overhangs the ends of the braces by about 5 mm. Space successive rows 10 mm apart by placing a spacer over each cross-brace. Use slats at least 2 metres long and work outwards from the centre of the slat, first to one end of the bench, then to the other, fastening the slat to each set of cross-braces with two 75 mm oval nails. On very long benches, where more than one slat is required to complete the curve, butt the slats together over a cross-brace. For a supply of spacers, rip cut several 50 by 25 mm boards into thin strips 10 mm wide, then cut the strips into 110 mm sections.

When all the slats are in place, reinforce the outside slats at each cross-brace by driving a 50 mm wood screw through the slats into the spacers. Then trim the slats at the ends of the bench in a straight line, and cap the trimmed slats with a 50 by 25 mm board, driving a 50 mm wood screw through the cap into every other slat *(inset)*.

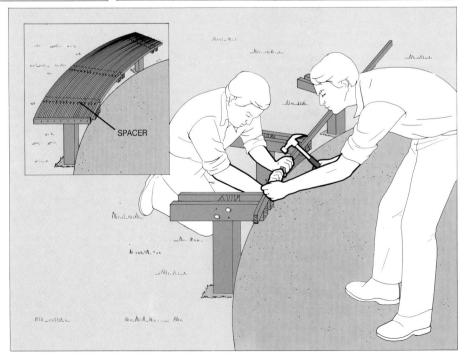

Plastic Furniture from Lightweight Tubing

Three all-purpose plastic pieces. The chair, footstool and side table shown here are all made of rigid PVC (plastic) pipe—36 mm pipe for the chair, 22 mm pipe for the footstool and table. They are joined with cross, elbow and T-fittings of the same material. The measurements given for each pipe section are based on standard sizes for the three pieces of furniture, but the sizes may vary to suit your needs. When calculating pipe lengths, subtract the length of the connecting fitting but add the depth of the fitting socket at each end of the pipe. When two fittings butt together, join them with a piece of pipe equal in length to two socket depths.

On the chair and footstool, canvas slings, sewn to fit around horizontal crosspieces, support removable cushions *(inset)*. The two-piece sling for the seat and back of the chair is stitched together at a line 175 mm from the back crosspiece.

Joining pipes and fittings. Cut all pipe sections at once, using the measurements given in the drawings above, and fit the parts together loosely in a dry run. Work on a flat surface so that parallel joints are square. For a chair, assemble the side sections first, then add the crosspieces for the seat and back. When the piece is complete, use a trimming knife to scratch a guideline across the pipe and fitting at each joint *(inset)*; the marks will speed reassembly as you glue the parts together. Dismantle the parts.

Working in a well-ventilated area and following the same sequence used in the dry run, glue all the parts together except the crosspieces that support the canvas slings. Spread pipe solvent cement on the inner lip of each fitting and slip the pipe into the fitting, tapping it with a rubber mallet if necessary for a snug fit. Hold each joint together for 30 seconds, until the glue has set. Attach the crosspieces for the canvas sling last, but do not glue them. Drill pilot holes through an inconspicuous spot on each joint, and screw the joints together with 12 mm wood screws, so that they can be taken apart and the canvas slings removed for washing.

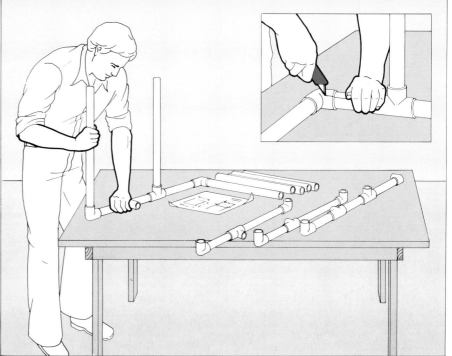

A Sun Space to Live in: Building a Conservatory

No longer the crystal palaces of the well-to-do, modern conservatories are usually of simple design and can be built on to almost any convenient wall. They function both as porches and as an extra living space, providing all-round shelter with maximum natural light, and their glazed walls and roof trap solar heat so effectively that on a sunny winter day the temperature inside can reach 30°C—even when it is below freezing outdoors.

To take full advantage of the sun's warmth, you will have to position the conservatory against the house wall that receives the most sunlight during the day. So that sunlight can penetrate the full depth of the structure, the side walls should be no more than half as long as the front wall. Local building regulations will almost certainly contain specific requirements concerning ventilation, drainage and other factors that may affect your design, so you should consult your local planning officer and building inspector at an early stage in your planning.

Professional advice is particularly important for the concrete slab that constitutes the base of the new structure and must bear its weight. The slab shown on the following pages is enclosed by concrete blocks, built on top of a level footing, which provide a solid foundation to which the conservatory walls can be directly attached. The footing must rest at or below the subsoil frost line and the slab must incorporate a damp-proof membrane at or below the level of the DPC in the house wall.

Services to the house such as cables, water pipes and drains may have to be re-routed to make way for the foundation.

For both the footing of the strip foundation and the reinforced slab, use concrete mixed in proportions of 1 part cement to 6 parts ballast. The footing can be built up with frost-resistant bricks, solid concrete blocks or hollow blocks filled with concrete after they are laid.

The walls of the conservatory are of standard stud construction; they are assembled on the ground and glazed after erection. A sliding door in the front wall provides the best combination of light and ventilation. Because doorframes vary in size, measure the one you will actually be using before drawing up detailed plans, and adjust the spacing between studs to allow for the doorframe.

The pitch of the roof is largely determined by the position of the existing first-floor windows. The steeper the pitch, the more sunlight the roof will catch in winter when the sun's arc is low in the sky; too great a pitch, however, will cause rainwater to overshoot the gutter, and could cause the glazing panels to slide down from their original positions. A difference in height of 450 mm between the front and back of the roof is usually sufficient.

Make the wooden framework for the walls and roof of the conservatory from cedar, redwood or pressure-treated timber; apply an extra coat of wood preservative before assembling the frame. Stain or paint the completed frame before glazing.

The roof is the most vulnerable part of the structure. It must admit sunlight, yet resist hailstorms and melting snow without breaking or leaking. Double-walled, 10 mm-thick sheets of acrylic offer virtually the same light transmission and insulating qualities as double-glazed glass panels, yet are far tougher. They are also lighter, which makes them safer and easier to install. Because acrylic expands and contracts in response to temperature changes to a greater extent than glass, the panels are installed in a special aluminium frame *(page 76)* fitted with rubber gaskets that form a tight yet flexible seal against water leakage.

Plastic guttering to collect the rainwater shed by the sloping roof is available as prefabricated components for assembly according to the manufacturer's instructions *(page 80)*. Use angled sections of guttering and downpipe to channel the rainwater back to a house drain. Alternatively, if no drain is located conveniently, route the rainwater via a downpipe and an underground drainage pipe to a soakaway—a rubble-filled pit that collects the water and lets it slowly percolate into the soil.

The choice of finishing materials for the floor of the completed structure includes tiles *(pages 40–46)*, flagstones *(pages 47–49)* and a plain mortar screed *(page 81)*. To avoid damage from exposure to overnight frost and rain, the job of veneering the concrete slab is best carried out after the walls and roof of the conservatory have been erected and glazed.

Anatomy of a conservatory. Attached to the house wall that receives the most sunlight, the 100 by 50 mm framework of a conservatory rests on a reinforced and damp-proofed concrete slab. The sole plates of the walls are formed from lengths of 150 by 75 mm wooden sill cut to size, on top of which 100 by 50 mm studs are set at 600 mm centres. The walls are held together at the corners by sturdy 100 by 100 mm posts, and a second layer of head plates gives the structure added rigidity. The triangular sections between the roof and side walls are sheathed with 18 mm exterior-grade plywood.

The roof is covered by acrylic panels mounted in aluminium frames set on 150 by 50 mm rafters. The walls are glazed with thick safety glass set between the studs. Access to the outdoors is through a sliding patio door.

Plastic guttering is attached with brackets to a fascia board at the top of the front wall; the downpipe is fitted with an angled shoe that channels the water away from the concrete slab.

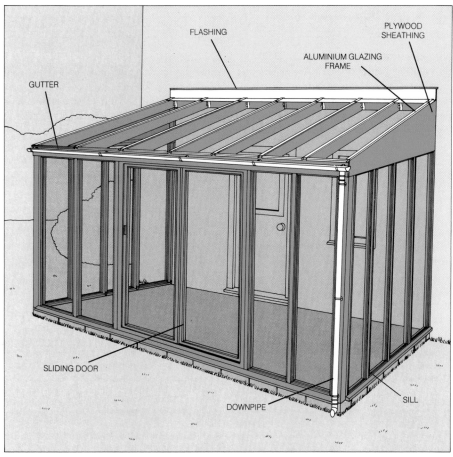

Anatomy of a strip foundation. Below or on a level with the frost line, a 200 mm-deep reinforced concrete footing is built in a 600 mm-wide trench around the perimeter of the slab to provide a solid base for the foundation. Laid centrally on the footing are courses of hollow concrete blocks filled with concrete; the top of the final course of blocks is 150 mm above ground level. The area within the blockwork is excavated 300 mm below the final course of blocks, then filled with a 150 mm layer of hardcore and a 25 mm sand blinding. DPC strips laid on top of the concrete blocks and an overlapping polythene membrane laid on top of the sand blinding are both tied in with the DPC in the house wall. The 100 mm-thick reinforced concrete slab is finished with a mortar screed, which constitutes the floor of the structure built over the slab.

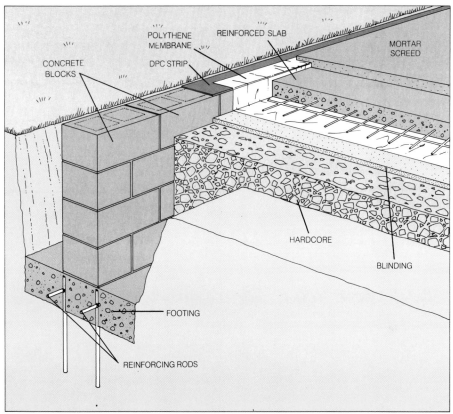

Building a Strip Foundation

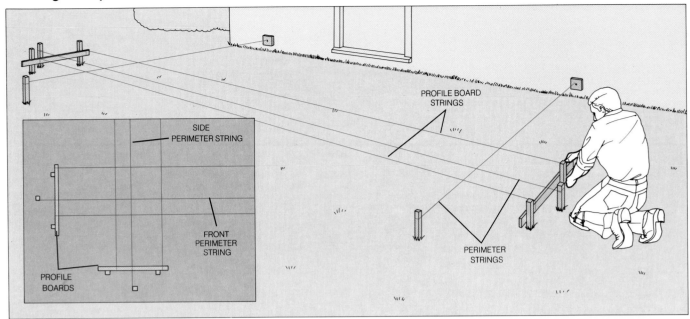

SIDE PERIMETER STRING

FRONT PERIMETER STRING

PROFILE BOARDS

PROFILE BOARD STRINGS

PERIMETER STRINGS

1 **Setting up profile boards.** Mark out the perimeter of the slab as described on page 9, positioning the stakes at least 1200 mm beyond the planned slab dimensions and attaching the side strings to scrap timbers nailed or screwed to the house wall. Level the strings 150 mm above ground level and mark the stakes at the exact height the strings are attached. At each end of the front perimeter string drive in two stakes 300 mm on either side of the string about 1 metre outside the side strings. Nail a 900 mm-long piece of 50 by 25 mm timber across each pair of stakes; in each of these profile boards, saw one notch 200 mm outside the perimeter string and a second notch 400 mm inside the string, then tie strings from the notches in one profile board to the notches in the opposite board (above). Set up profile boards and strings along the sides of the slab site in the same way (inset), attaching the strings to the house wall with masonry nails.

2 **Preparing the trench.** Draw chalk lines on the ground directly beneath the strings attached to the profile boards, then remove the profile boards and strings and also the perimeter guide strings. Excavate the trench to the required depth within the chalk lines, and remove all topsoil from the slab area enclosed by the trench. To install level pegs for the top of the footing, drive in lengths of reinforcing rod along the bottom of the trench at 1 metre intervals and 200 mm from each side. Using the method described on page 86, have a helper hold one end of a spirit level against the 150 mm mark on one of the perimeter stakes, and measure down from the other end of the level to establish the correct height for the footing. Tie the spirit level to a long straightedge if necessary. The vertical distance between the spirit level and the top of the level pegs must equal the height of the number of block courses required to rise from the top of the footing to 150 mm above ground level. Adjust the first level peg as necessary, then level the remaining pegs to the height of the first.

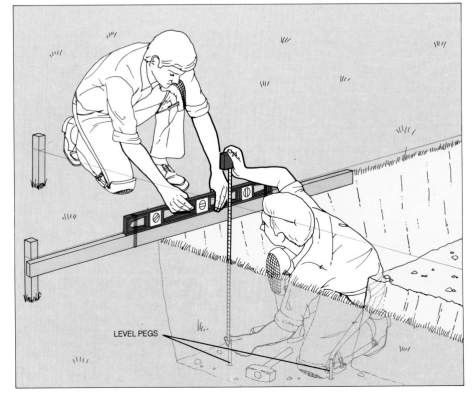

LEVEL PEGS

3 **Pouring the footing.** Tie horizontal lengths of reinforcing rod along each row of level pegs about 75 mm from the trench floor. Pour concrete into the trench until it is about 10 mm above the peg tops, digging in with a shovel to eliminate air bubbles, then compact the concrete with a tamping beam with handles attached and level it to the exact height of the level pegs. Allow the concrete footing to cure for 48 hours, then lay joint filler strips against the house wall at the ends of the side trenches.

4 **Building the foundation wall.** Reattach the perimeter strings to their stakes and mark chalk lines in the footing directly beneath them. Lay a dry run of hollow concrete blocks along the chalk lines and adjust the width of the joints between them as necessary; to check for adjustment to the joints between courses, measure from the perimeter strings down to the footing. Remove the strings, then build up the ends and corners of the foundation wall with stepped courses of hollow concrete blocks to the required height above ground. Use lines strung between the stepped ends and corners as guides for filling in the sides and front of the wall *(page 92, Step 1)*. Check for level and plumb as you work, and fill the hollow blocks with concrete as each course is completed.

5 **Laying the DPC.** Excavate the area enclosed by the strip foundation to a depth of 300 mm below the top of the concrete blocks. Place strips of joint filler against the house wall. Fill in the area with a 150 mm layer of hardcore and a 25 mm sand blinding, and backfill the trench on the outside of the blocks with the soil that was removed from the trench. Along the top of the concrete blocks, bed strips of DPC in a thin layer of mortar, lapping the ends of the strips up the house wall to a height of 25 mm above the house DPC. Lay sheets of 1000-gauge polythene across the sand blinding, overlapping joints by 150 mm and overlapping the DPC on the blocks by 100 mm. Allow a 25 mm excess above the house DPC along the house wall.

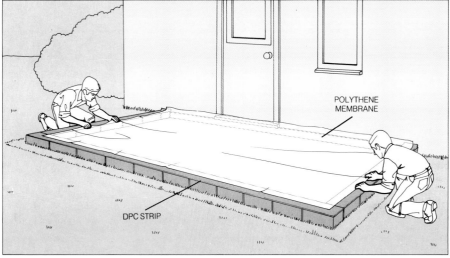

POLYTHENE MEMBRANE

DPC STRIP

6 Tying in the DPC to the house. Lay sheets of 6 mm 200 by 200 mm wire mesh supported on spacers on top of the polythene, leaving a 50 mm gap round the edges and taking special care not to puncture the polythene *(page 13)*.

Pour, tamp and skip-float a 100 mm slab of concrete on top of the polythene as described on pages 17–18, and leave to cure.

Using a club hammer and bolster, chip out a course of mortar along the house wall at the height of the DPC and to a depth of 35 mm. Press the edges of the DPC strips and the polythene membrane into the gap to join up with the house DPC, and secure the joint with mastic.

Constructing the Walls

1 Marking the slab. Using a piece of 100 by 50 mm timber as a measure, mark a line 100 mm in from each edge of the block wall. At one end of the slab, hold the timber upright at the point where the marked line meets the wall of the house and check it for vertical with a plumb bob; then, while a helper holds the timber in position, continue the line up the wall to the planned height of the stud framework *(right)*. Mark the wall at the other end of the slab in the same way.

2 Marking the sill and head plate. For each side wall, cut a piece of 150 by 75 mm timber sill to the length of one side of blockwork less 100 mm and lay it on the ground. Use a steel square to mark locations for 50 mm-thick studs at each end of the sill, then mark further stud locations along the sill at regular centres of not more than 600 mm. Cut a piece of 100 by 50 mm timber 100 mm longer than the sill to act as a head plate and lay it alongside the sill on 25 mm-thick scrap blocks of wood. While a helper holds the head plate aligned with one end of the sill, use the steel square to transfer the stud location marks on the sill to the head plate *(right)*.

For the front wall, cut both sill and head plate to the length of the blockwork less 200 mm. Mark stud locations as for the side walls, leaving a sufficient gap in the centre of the wall to allow for the sliding door.

3 **Securing the studs and corner posts.** Lay the studs for one side wall on edge and set the head plate above them with its location marks facing the studs. Line up each stud with a location mark, and drive two 100 mm nails through the plate into the stud. Attach the sill in the same manner, then assemble the framework for the second side wall and the front wall.

To make the corner posts, cut two pieces of 100 by 100 mm timber 75 mm longer than the studs. Fix them to each side wall by nailing through the projecting section of the head plate into the top of the post, then screwing into the side of the post from the end stud *(inset)*.

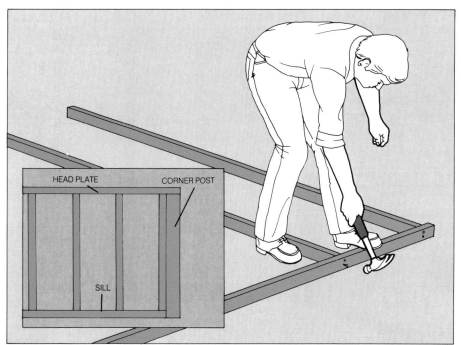

HEAD PLATE   CORNER POST

SILL

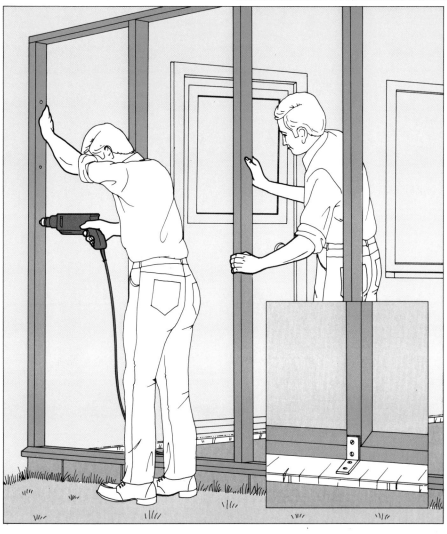

4 **Securing the side walls.** With a helper, raise a side-wall framework on to the concrete blocks. Rest the sill on the DPC strip and align the inside edge of the end stud with the mark on the wall. While the helper holds the framework in place, drill through the end stud and 50 mm into the wall at 300 mm intervals; if the wall surface is uneven or not plumb, insert packing between the wall and the stud at the drilling positions. Secure the framework to the wall with 100 mm frame fasteners, then attach the other side-wall framework in the same manner.

Bolt both side sections to the concrete blocks with angle brackets screwed into the sill and studs *(inset)*. Alternatively, drive 100 mm frame fasteners directly through the sill midway between each pair of studs.

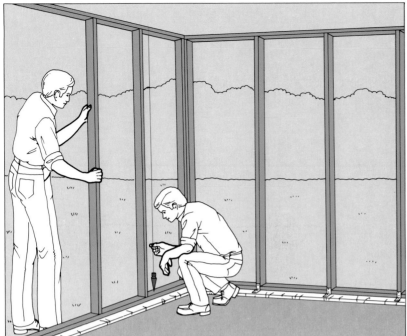

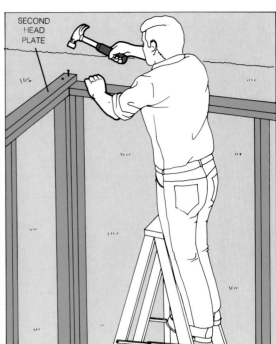

5 **Aligning the front wall.** Lift the front-wall framework into position on the concrete blocks and align it with the corner posts. Drive a nail part way into the inside of the head plate near the end stud and hang a plumb bob from it, with the tip of the bob level with the top of the sill. Have a helper move the wall gradually towards the vertical. When the tip of the bob lines up with the edge of the sill, drill and screw through the end stud into the corner post. Align the other corner in the same way, then secure the framework to the concrete blocks as for the side walls.

6 **Adding the second head plate.** Cut a piece of 100 by 50 mm timber to the length of the front wall. Lay the new head plate in position on the first one, overlapping the ends of the side-wall head plates, and secure it with staggered 75 mm nails, one between every pair of studs. Cut similar pieces of timber to fit between the new head plate and the walls of the house, and nail them to the original head plates of the side walls.

7 **Attaching the beading.** Cut and mitre strips of timber beading to fit around the inside of each stud frame flush with the outer faces of the studs. Using waterproof PVA adhesive, glue and pin the bottom beading strip to the sill. Attach the side and top strips in the same way, making sure they are plumb with the lower strip and that the inner faces are flush at the corners.

Adding the Roof Framework

1 **Attaching the ledger.** Cut a 150 by 50 mm ledger as long as the front wall of the conservatory, and drill 9 mm holes at 450 mm intervals. Mark the intended location of the ledger on the house wall by measuring 300 mm up from each side-wall head plate, then snap a chalk line across the wall and drive a masonry nail part way into the wall at each end. With a helper, raise the ledger, rest it on the protruding nails and mark the fixing positions on the wall. Lower the ledger, remove the protruding nails and drill 15 mm holes in the wall at the marked positions. Secure the ledger with 100 mm expanding anchor bolts, inserting all the bolts first, then tightening each one with a spanner.

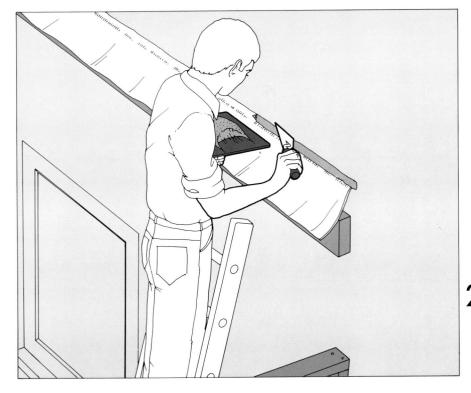

2 **Installing the flashing.** Using a bolster chisel and club hammer, chop out a course of mortar no more than 100 mm above the ledger to a depth of 25 mm. Push the edge of a 225 mm-wide flashing strip into the gap along the length of the ledger. Bend the flashing strip down to the top of the ledger, then secure the strip in the wall with mortar (left).

3 Making a template for the rafters. Mark a centre line down the face of a 150 by 50 mm board. While a helper holds the lower end of the board so that the centre line touches the outer corner of the side-wall head plate, butt the upper end against the house wall with its face against the end of the ledger. Hold the top corner of the 150 by 50 mm board level with the top corner of the ledger and mark it with a pair of compasses: set one leg against the vertical face of the ledger and draw the compasses downwards so that the other leg scribes a parallel line on the 150 by 50 mm board. Take the board down and cut it along the line with a circular saw. Butt the cut end against the front of the ledger, and trace the shape of the side-wall head plate on to the lower end. Extend the lines *(inset)* and cut the 150 by 50 mm board along the lines. Using this board as a template, mark and cut all the rafters required for the roof.

EXTENDED CUT
LINES

CENTRE
LINE

HEAD-PLATE
MARKS

4 Hanging the rafters. Nail a 100 by 50 mm board flat against the house wall at each end of the conservatory between the ledger and the side-wall head plate. Then install the rafters, spacing them at centres no more than 600 mm apart, their lower ends over the front wall studs. Secure each rafter to the ledger and the front-wall head plate with truss clips, nailing into the timbers through the metal flanges.

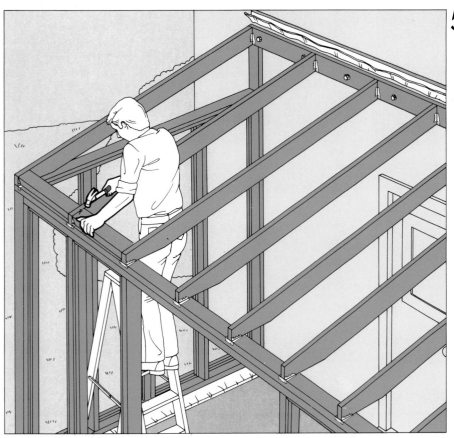

5 **Installing roof blocking.** Toenail a 100 by 50 mm block between each pair of rafters at the front-wall head plate to form a continuous flat surface as a base for the roof glazing. Angle each section of blocking so that its face is flush with the top faces of the rafters and its outermost corner is even with the rafter ends.

Condensation may run down the underside of the roof glazing. To prevent it from collecting on the interior horizontal surface of the front-wall head plate, fill the V-shaped spaces between the blocking and the head plate with 100 by 50 mm blocks bevelled to fit, creating a vertical surface that will shed water away from the head plate.

6 **Enclosing the triangular sections.** From a sheet of 18 mm exterior-grade plywood, cut a triangular section to cover the area between the bottom of a side-wall head plate and the top of an end rafter. Nail it to the rafter, head plate and the vertical timber beneath the end of the ledger; space the nails every 150 mm along the edge of the plywood. Cut and secure a second triangular section to the opposite side wall, then nail a length of 100 by 25 mm board along the head plates of the front wall to act as a fascia for the guttering.

Glazing the Roof and Walls

For the roof—which should be glazed before the walls to minimize the risk of breaking a window pane—most of the glazing components are available as patented systems designed for roofing greenhouses and carports. The systems vary in design, but all work along the same principle *(right)*. Sold by builders' merchants and sheet-plastic distributors, the acrylic glazing panels come in sizes of up to 3000 by 990 mm, and can be cut with a fine-toothed saw; alternatively, they can be ordered to size. When calculating the length required, remember to allow for a 25 mm overhang into the gutter.

For glazing the walls, use tempered safety glass. Measure the height and width of each section of the stud framework carefully, and subtract 3 mm from these dimensions to allow for expansion and contractions within the frame.

Sliding doors for access from outside are available in kit form for assembly on site *(page 79)*. The frames come in timber, aluminium or plastic, and can be ordered to size if you have not based your conservatory plan on a specific standard size.

After installing guttering and downpipes to channel away rainwater shed by the sloping roof *(page 80)*, caulk the joints between the house wall and the conservatory with a non-hardening sealant. Insulated roller blinds will conserve heat during the cold winter nights, and pull-down shades on the roof will provide protection against the glare of the summer sun.

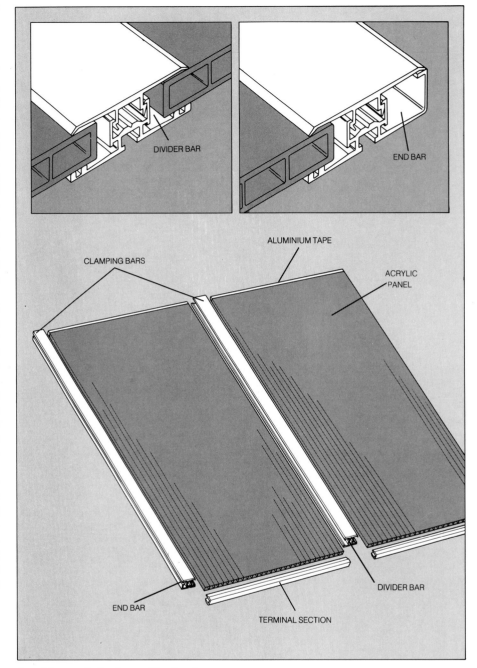

DIVIDER BAR

END BAR

ALUMINIUM TAPE

CLAMPING BARS

ACRYLIC PANEL

END BAR

TERMINAL SECTION

DIVIDER BAR

Assembling a glazing frame. The framing sections of this rooftop glazing system comprise aluminium end bars that form the side edges of the framework, aluminium divider bars with rubber gaskets that support adjoining panel edges, and rigid plastic clamping bars that sandwich the panel edges against the divider bars *(left inset)* and end bars *(right inset)*. A U-shaped aluminium terminal section with weepholes for condensation drainage covers the lower end of each panel, while the tops are sealed with aluminium adhesive tape. The framework is screwed to the rafters through holes drilled along the centre line of the end and divider bars. The double-walled 10 mm-thick acrylic glazing panels contain insulating air cavities, and are covered with a protective masking which is removed after installation.

Fastening the Frame to the Roof

1 **Mounting the first glazing bar.** Mark a line down the centre of the top face of one end rafter. Align the screw holes in the bottom half of an end bar over the line, the upper end of the bar flush with the upper end of the rafter, and clamp the bar to the rafter. Screw the bar in position. Remove the cramps and attach an end bar to the opposite end rafter and divider bars to intermediate rafters in the same fashion.

2 **Glazing the roof.** Seal the top end of an acrylic glazing panel with aluminium tape and clip the terminal section on to the lower end. Position the panel between the first pair of glazing bars, allowing about 3 mm either side for expansion; the bottom of the panel should overhang the fascia board by 25 mm. Place a clamping bar over the panel and clip it on to the end bar. Working from between the third and fourth rafters, lay the second panel in position, then lean across it and clip a clamping bar on to the divider bar separating the two panels. Glaze the rest of the roof in this way, peeling back the protective masking from each panel when it is gripped at either side by the glazing bars. Use a block of wood to press down the flashing on to the top of the panels as you proceed.

Glazing the Walls

1 Preparing the frame. Soften a handful of linseed oil putty by kneading it in your hands. If necessary, add linseed oil to make it more pliant. Holding the putty in the palm of your hand, use your thumb to press a continuous strip about 3 mm thick along the inside of the glazing beads around one of the frames. Press two setting blocks into the putty at the bottom of the frame to help support the weight of the glass.

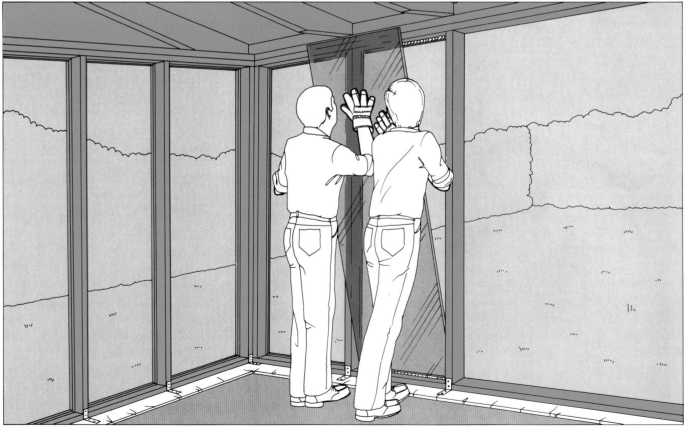

2 Setting the glass. With a helper, lift up a pane of glass and rest its base on the setting blocks. Press the pane gently against the glazing beads, increasing the pressure until the glass is firmly secured in the putty. Remove any excess putty from the inside of the pane with the blade of a knife. Cut and mitre lengths of glazing bead to fit round the inside of the glazed section; for easy removal of the glass in case of breakage, secure the beading with panel pins only, not with adhesive.

Installing the Sliding Door

1 **Fixing the frame.** Assemble the frame on the ground according to the manufacturer's instructions. With a helper, lift the frame into the opening in the wall. Use a spirit level to check that it is plumb and square and, if necessary, insert packing between the frame and the studs. Drill countersunk fixing holes through the frame and into the studs, then screw the frame to the studs and fill the holes with wood filler.

2 **Installing the stationary panel.** Place the upper edge of the stationary panel in the channel at the top of the frame and drop the lower edge into the bottom channel, sliding it firmly against the jamb. Place the threshold step in the slot in the sill between the bottom of the panel and the opposite jamb, and screw it in position *(right)*. Secure the head closer in the top of the frame in the same way.

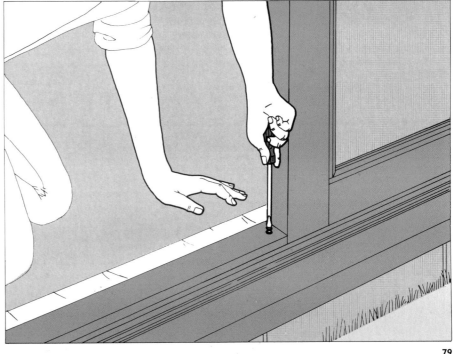

3 **Fitting the sliding panel.** Working from outside the conservatory, push the top of the sliding panel on to the upper track guide inside the top of the frame *(right)*. Swing the panel inwards so that it rests in the lower track. Secure the head and sill stops in the upper and lower tracks. Open and close the door to check the sliding action, and correct the clearance by adjusting the rollers at the bottom of the sliding door according to the manufacturer's instructions.

Attaching Plastic Guttering

Securing the gutter at an incline. Stretch a level string between nails at either end of the fascia board, then lower the string at one end to mark an incline for the gutter of not less than 5 mm in 3 metres. Mark positions for support brackets at intervals recommended by the manufacturer, then remove the string. Secure the brackets to the fascia board, and clip the guttering into the brackets *(right)*. To connect consecutive sections, use clips lined with rubber gaskets or jointing cement as instructed by the manufacturer.

If a soakaway has been prepared, secure an outlet section at the lower end of the guttering and attach a downpipe and shoe to the corner post with support brackets. To channel the rainwater to a drain outside the house wall, use a corner angle section, then run guttering across the plywood sheathing to an outlet section attached to angled sections of downpipe which lead across the house wall to the drain.

Laying a Level Mortar Screed

Because of its dry, crumbly texture, a sand and cement screed must be laid in manageable sections to ensure a level surface. Timber battens bedded in strips of mortar and levelled to the planned height of the finished floor are used to divide the floor area into bays no wider than 1 metre; after each bay is filled and smoothed, you can reach across to remove the batten no longer needed and fill in the gap.

The order in which the bays are filled depends on the position of the room exit. In the conservatory shown here, the final bay must be filled from a scaffold board or ladder bridge *(page 18)* laid between the doorways of the house and conservatory.

The screed mortar consists of a mix of 1 part cement to 3 parts sharp sand. The consistency is correct when a ball of mortar held in the hand holds its shape when released, but just begins to crack apart. For a strong bond between the screed and a cured concrete slab, dampen the slab 24 hours before laying the screed and brush on a liquid paste of cement and water just before bedding the timber battens.

1 **Dividing the room into bays.** At one side of the slab, lay a 150 mm-wide strip of screed mortar. About 50 mm from the inside face of the block work, bed a 50 by 25 mm batten in the mortar, wide face up, and check for level—the upper face of the batten should be 25 mm above the level of the blockwork. Trowel mortar between the batten and side sill, tamp with a length of timber, then smooth with a float. Repeat on the opposite side of the slab, ensuring that the two battens are level. Then lay 100 mm-wide strips of screed mortar at intervals of about 1 metre across the slab and bed 50 by 25 mm battens in them. Ensure that all the battens are level and flush.

2 **Finishing the screed.** Shovel mortar into an empty bay adjacent to one of the outermost battens until it reaches about 10 mm above the battens. Compact the mortar by tamping with a length of timber, then draw the timber along the tops of the battens with a zigzag motion to scrape off the excess. Smooth the levelled mortar and fill in shallow depressions with a wood float, then polish with a steel float. Reach over the completed section and prise out the batten farthest from the finished edge, then fill in and level the hole. Fill and level the remaining bays in the same way. Cover the screed with polythene and leave to cure for three days.

3

Walls and Arches of Brick and Stone

Dressing down a rock. A wide-bladed stone chisel and a 2 kilogram club hammer—two essentials of a stonemason's tool kit—are used together to split and dress blocks of quarried granite. Light taps of the hammer against the chisel score a cutting line; then increasingly sharper blows slice and trim the rock along its grain into building blocks for stone walls or arches.

However imposing the finished structure, a building made of brick, block or stone rises in manageable increments, on a comfortably human scale. Walls of almost limitless bulk and weight are composed of masonry units that a single worker can lift, and they are bonded together with mortar, a concoction so prosaic that masons often call it "muck". Even the skills essential to masonry are simple: one twist of the wrist spreads mortar in an even bed, another twist "butters" an individual component and a third settles it into place.

But if individual bricks, blocks and stones are simple to lift and mortar together, no one should underestimate their bulk and complexity en masse. A single brick is manageable; a 1 tonne cube of 400 bricks delivered at the front of a house for a building project in the back garden poses a challenge equivalent to moving a small mountain. And although one brick laid slightly askew in a rising wall may pass unnoticed, the sum of many small misalignments is an unsightly and potentially unstable structure.

To ensure that the apparent simplicity of the work does not lead to pitfalls, advance planning is essential. For many masonry projects, the planning will inevitably involve a certain amount of paperwork. When brick or stone is being used to sheathe an existing wall, for example, every dimension of the new wall has to duplicate the dimensions of the wall being covered—and this requirement often means that even the thickness of the mortar joints must be calculated ahead of time. For decorative brickwork, a sketch that charts the patterns and shifts of colour will provide an invaluable guide when you are laying the bricks. And for an arch or a serpentine wall, you will have to employ some basic principles of geometry to design the curved plywood template against which the bricks will fit.

Preliminary planning can also help you cope with the weight and vol- the courses of masonry rising straight and true. In most cases this is done with racked "stopped ends" built at opposite ends of the planned wall—several courses of bricks or blocks that rise in stepped courses from ground level at either end of the wall. The mason's line that is stretched between the stopped ends acts as a guide for the placement of all the intervening bricks.

Preliminary planning can also help you cope with the weight and volume of masonry materials. Before the bricks, blocks or stones arrive, set up a routine with your helper or helpers. Typically, professional masons arrange to have small stacks of materials distributed along the wall they are erecting—piles of 40 to 50 bricks, or eight to 10 blocks or stones, placed about 2 metres apart and about 600 mm back from the wall—with full boards of mortar interspersed between the stacks. The mason is thus never out of reach of the supplies, which are kept constantly replenished by helpers.

Constructing Solid Footings for Garden Walls

A wall is only as strong as the footing it stands on. This long concrete strip carries the weight of the wall down to the solid, unexcavated soil below the frost line. In addition, a footing performs two other crucial jobs: its level top provides a firm, flat surface on which to build, and its width, which is greater than that of the wall itself, spreads the load over a larger area.

Even the construction of a garden wall is likely to be governed by building or planning regulations, so you should contact your local council before planning the project in detail. In particular, they will be able to advise you on the correct depth for the footing, which will vary according to the type of soil and the level of the subsoil frost line. In the case of a boundary between your property and an adjoining one, the wall must be built on your side of the boundary line. If planning permission is required, prepare a scale drawing of the project to accompany your application.

The next step is to transfer your plan from paper to the building site, using stakes and string to mark out the lines and levels. A properly prepared site will not only save time and money, but it may also forestall potential structural problems. Wherever possible, the dimensions of footings and foundation walls should be based on those of modular building materials, such as standard concrete blocks or bricks; if the site is incorrectly set out, the modules will have to be cut and the bonding pattern in which they are laid may be affected.

Use the 3-4-5 method to square corners *(page 9)* and a water level to establish elevations *(page 86)*. You can buy a professional water level from a builders' merchant, or you can make your own with a length of clear, flexible tubing and a funnel. A water level is accurate over any distance and can be used round corners or obstacles. Make sure, however, that there are no air bubbles in the tube—these can lead to false readings.

In the case of a long wall, or where the wall is to be sited on a slope, it is more convenient to do the setting out with an automatic level and a levelling staff—a wooden or aluminium pole with graduated markings. The simple automatic level of the type shown on page 88 can be hired, together with a tripod and levelling staff, from a surveying firm.

On sloping ground, the footing should be stepped, with each step rising in multiples of your walling unit. For brick walls, the most convenient unit for this purpose is 225 mm, the height of three bricks and mortar courses; for block walls, measure in units of a single block height plus a mortar course. The horizontal distance between steps is not crucial, but for structural reasons it should be at least 1 metre.

Guide strings stretched between wooden frames known as profile boards are used to establish the outline of the foundation trench *(opposite page)*. The width of the trench depends on the width of the footings, and this, in turn, is determined by the height of the wall. A footing at least twice the width of the masonry is acceptable for most walls under 750 mm high; for walls over 750 mm, the footing should be three times the width.

A footing must be at least 250 mm deep, and it must rest on or below the subsoil frost line. The top of the footing should be 50 to 150 mm below ground level—this means that the edges of the footing will be covered in soil, leaving sufficient room for you to dig and plant next to the wall.

Where the soil is compact and stable, the trench dug for the footing can itself serve as a form for the concrete, and level pegs driven into the trench floor will indicate the height to which the concrete for the footing must be poured *(page 86)*. Where the soil is unstable, you will need wooden form boards to shape the concrete and establish the footing height *(page 87)*. For a stepped footing on a sloping site, you will also need to install baffles—special form boards made of 12 mm plywood which are used to shape the vertical edge of the concrete at each step *(page 88)*.

Where form boards are used, the foundation trench must be dug about 400 mm wider and longer than the footing to allow room for setting up the boards and their supporting stakes. The gap between the form boards and the sides of the trench should be packed with earth before the concrete is poured.

With the form boards or level pegs in place, carry out any reinforcement work that may be required by local building regulations, using lines of 10 mm steel rods raised about 75 mm from the floor of the trench *(page 87)*. The rods can be cut with bolt croppers or a hacksaw. For corners and stepped footings, use a length of metal pipe as a sleeve for bending the rods to the required shape.

Having completed the excavation work, you can arrange for delivery of the concrete *(page 17)*. Explain what you need the concrete for, bearing in mind that the mix for a stepped footing needs to be stiffer than that for a normal footing. Arrange for the concrete to be unloaded as close to the site as possible, and have several helpers on hand—it takes about 25 wheelbarrow-loads to shift a single cubic metre.

Setting Out on a Level Site

1 Notching the profile boards. Drive in a stake about 2 metres beyond each end of the proposed wall to mark the centre line, then run a string between them just above ground level. One metre in from each stake, drive in two more stakes well outside the intended working area and at equal distances from the centre line. About 200 mm above the ground, nail a level 50 by 25 mm board across each pair of stakes.

Using a plumb bob or spirit level, mark the centre line of the wall on the tops of the profile boards; measure out from here to the width of the wall itself, and then out again to the width of the footing, nicking each location with a saw to provide an anchor for strings (inset). In loose or sandy soil, cut two extra notches, one on each side of the footing, as guides for installing form boards (page 87). Remove the centre line string.

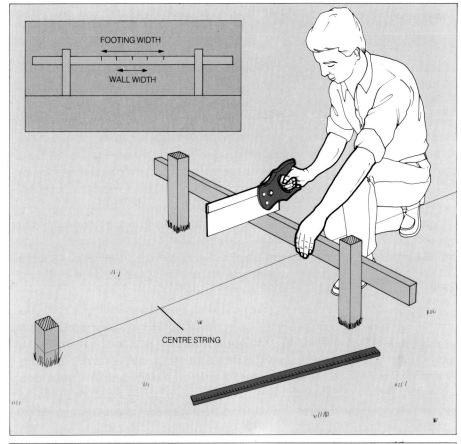

FOOTING WIDTH

WALL WIDTH

CENTRE STRING

2 Marking the guide lines. Stretch string lines between the outer notches on the profile boards. Fill a plastic squeeze bottle with chalk, and trim the bottle top at an angle to produce a wide line. Dispense a line of chalk on the ground directly beneath each string line. Remove the strings for excavation, but leave the profile boards in place.

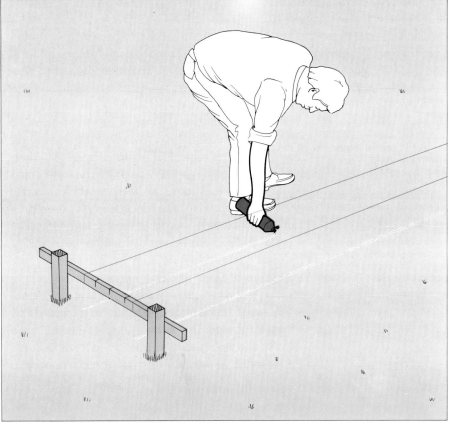

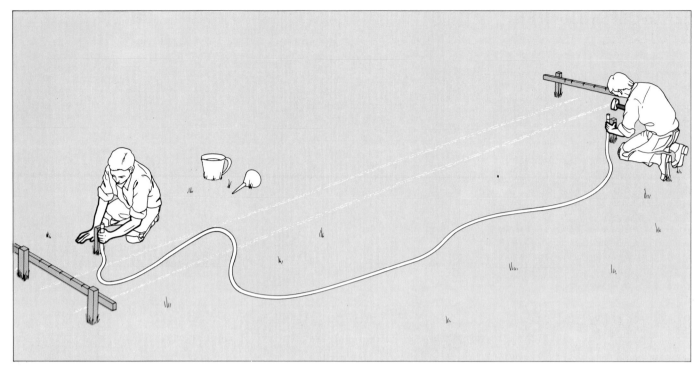

3 **Installing datum pegs.** To establish a precise level from which to measure down to the top of the footing, first drive in a 50 mm square stake at one corner of the projected trench, about 300 mm from the edge, leaving about 150 mm above ground. Drive in a second datum peg at the other end of the trench on the opposite side. Have a helper hold one end of a water level against the first stake, aligning the level of the water in the hose with the stake top. Stretch the hose to the other stake. Drive in the top of the second stake until it is at the level of the water in the hose.

A Packed-Earth Form for Poured Concrete

Setting the level pegs. Dig out the trench to the required depth between the chalk lines. Cut lengths of 10 mm reinforcing rod to serve as level pegs for the footing. Set one peg about 75 mm in from either end of the trench and midway between the sides, and drive in the remaining pegs at 1 metre intervals down the length of the trench. If you are adding reinforcement *(opposite page, below)*, set the level pegs on either side of the trench so they can be used to support the horizontal rods.

While a helper holds one end of a spirit level on one of the datum pegs, measure down from the opposite end of the level the height of the datum peg above ground (150 mm) plus the planned depth of the footing surface below ground. Hammer down the first level peg to the correct height for the footing. Work your way to the opposite end of the trench, checking the level from one peg to the next and hammering down as necessary. Use the second datum peg to check the level of the last level peg in the row.

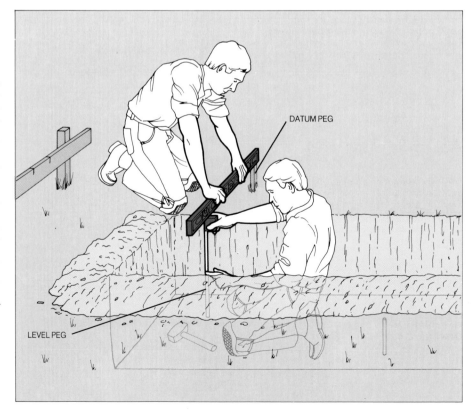

DATUM PEG

LEVEL PEG

Installing Form Boards for a Footing

Securing the boards. Tie string lines between the footing notches on the profile boards. At each end of the trench floor, hold a spirit level or plumb bob against the strings, measure out 12 mm towards the sides of the trench and drive in 50 mm stakes. Tie taut strings between the inside faces of the stakes as guides for installing further stakes at 1 metre intervals along both sides of the trench. Adjust the height of the stakes to the planned footing height by the method shown on the opposite page, below. Nail lengths of 12 mm plywood trimmed to the exact height of the footing to the inside faces of the stakes, ensuring that the tops of the stakes and boards are flush.

Building Curved Forms

Laying out stakes in a curve. Draw two parallel chalk lines down the middle of the trench, reproducing the excavation curves for a serpentine wall *(page 102)*. Space the lines as far apart as the width of the footing. Drive in 50 mm square support stakes 300 mm apart and the same distance outside the lines as the thickness of the form boards. Hammer down the stakes to the footing level, as described opposite.

Cut plywood to the height of the footing. For gentle curves, use 12 mm plywood; for tighter curves, two thicknesses of 5 mm plywood. Nail the plywood to the stakes, its top level with the tops of the stakes *(inset)*. Push earth about half way up the form boards to brace them.

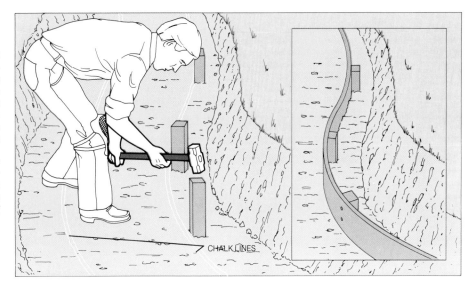

CHALK LINES

Adding Reinforcement

Providing horizontal support. Place lengths of reinforcing rod in two parallel lines along the floor of the trench, setting each line about 50 mm in from the proposed edge of the footing. In an earth-formed footing, fix the rods to the level pegs about 75 mm above the trench floor with steel tie wire. In a timber-formed footing, cut short pieces of rod for cross ties and fix them to the two parallel lines; space the cross ties about 1 metre apart, and set pieces of brick or small stones under the rods to lift them about 75 mm *(inset)*. Where lengths of rod join, overlap their ends about 400 mm for 10 mm rods, more for larger rods, and tie them together with tie wire.

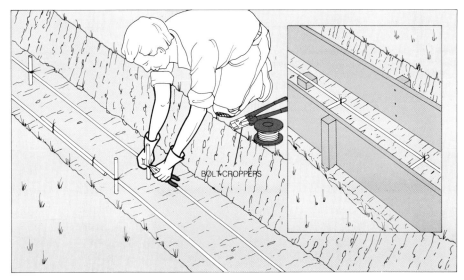

BOLT CROPPERS

Setting Out on a Slope

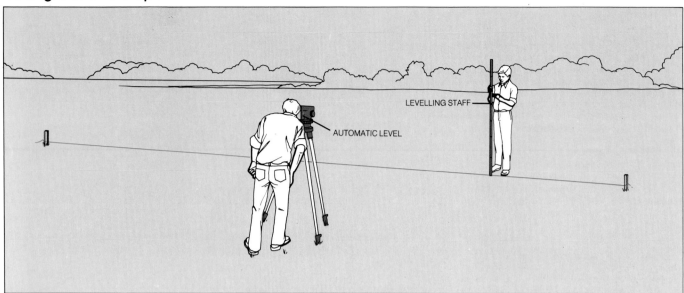

AUTOMATIC LEVEL

LEVELLING STAFF

1 Marking the steps. Drive in two stakes to mark the centre line of the proposed wall, and run a string between them. Set up an automatic level approximately midway between the stakes and about 1 to 2 metres to the side of the centre line string. Ask a helper to hold a levelling staff at the lower stake and adjust the crossbar until you see a continuous line through the eyepiece of the level. Note the reading on the levelling staff, then get your helper to move slowly up the slope while you continue to look through the eyepiece. Wherever the reading on the staff exceeds the previous reading by the height of your walling unit, get your helper to drive in a stake. As he passes you, rotate the level to face up the slope and repeat the process.

Starting at the foot of the slope, measure the distance between each stake. Wherever this is less than 1 metre, remove the uphill stake and mark the next stake to show that the level change at that point is equal to twice the height of your walling unit.

Set up profile boards and string lines using the method shown on page 85, and mark the outline of the trench with a plastic squeeze bottle filled with chalk. Chalk the outline of the edge of a step at each stake, then remove the stakes. Excavate the trench to the required level, dropping the trench floor by the required number of walling units at the outline of each step.

2 Placing the baffles. Measure 300 mm out from the vertical of each step, and chalk a line across the width of the trench. Drive support stakes diagonally into the side of the trench at each line; sink the stakes at least 300 mm into the earth, leaving about 200 mm protruding. Cut 12 mm plywood baffles, about 25 mm longer than the width of the trench and as wide as the steps are high. For the top step of the trench, double that height, so that the top of the baffle board will also serve as a level peg.

Set level pegs in the trench *(page 86)*, then wedge the baffles into the trench on the uphill side of the support stakes. Using a club hammer, force each baffle down until its lower edge is exactly aligned with the tops of the two preceding level pegs, and its upper edge with the top of the two succeeding level pegs. Hold a short level against the face of each baffle to check it for plumb, and against the upper edge to check it for level. Nail the baffles to their support stakes.

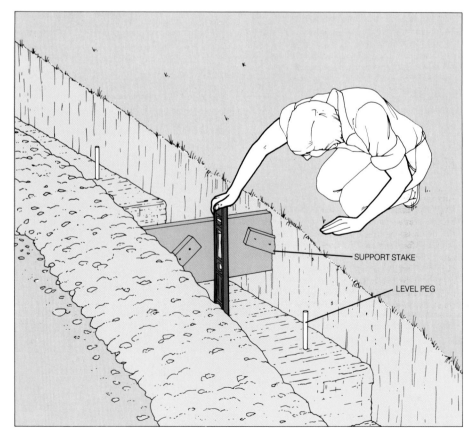

SUPPORT STAKE

LEVEL PEG

Pouring the Concrete

Laying a level footing. As you pour the concrete into the trench, have your helper spread it evenly between the trench walls or the form boards, using a square-ended shovel to compact the concrete and to force out air pockets. Continue pouring until the concrete reaches a few millimetres above the tops of the level pegs or forms.

Laying a stepped footing. Fill the lowest level of the trench to 10 mm above the top of the level pegs, using a shovel to push concrete under the first baffle. Tamp the concrete with a 100 by 50 mm timber beam and leave it to set for 10 to 15 minutes. Move to the downhill side of the second baffle and pour the next step. Push the concrete under the second baffle and pull it against the first baffle until it lines up with the top of the baffle and with the level pegs. Again, tamp the concrete and let it set for 10 to 15 minutes. Continue pouring and levelling the concrete into each step up the slope until the entire footing is laid.

Finishing the Footing

Tamping the surface. Use a 100 by 50 mm length of timber to tamp the concrete. With a helper at one end, work across the trench, lifting the beam up and down to compact the concrete *(right)*. After tamping the entire surface, remove any excess concrete above the level pegs by dragging the beam across the footing in a zigzag motion. When you finish, the tops of the level pegs should be barely visible at the surface of the concrete. Leave the surface coarse to provide a key for the mortar.

Brick Walls for the Garden: Variations on a Theme

A brick wall is above all else functional. But with variations of the conventional elements of bricklaying, a wall that defines a boundary or encloses a garden can also be decorative. In its simplest form, this secondary role rings the changes on the traditional bonds, or patterns, in which bricks are laid. Or it combines different coloured bricks. Bricks can also be offset from the wall plane to create contrapuntal effects of light and shadow, or to accentuate a corner with an architectural device called a rusticated quoin.

One decorative variant of brickwork is to make a lattice, screening an area while allowing breezes to pass through. Another is to break up the brick mass with graceful serpentine curves. Bricks can also be laid in a variety of patterns to finish a wall with an ornamental coping, and mortar joints can be tinted to vary their colour or specially tooled to vary their shape.

The basic bricklaying techniques are demonstrated opposite and overleaf in the construction of a plain freestanding wall. The pattern shown, in which courses of headers and stretchers alternate, is known as English bond. Stepped sections of brickwork are first built up at each end of the footing, and the wall is then raised course by course between them. In each course of headers, the correct geometric pattern of staggered vertical joints is achieved by laying "queen closers"—bricks split in half lengthwise—as the second and penultimate bricks.

The mortar that bonds the bricks together is made up of 1 part cement to 6 parts sand, mixed with water to the pliable consistency of soft butter. The mortar is laid—or "thrown"—with a trowel in a line about 500 mm long, and the point of the trowel is then used to make a shallow furrow along its centre. After the first brick has been set, subsequent bricks are "buttered" with mortar along the end or side to be set against the previous brick.

As well as a trowel and spirit level, you will need a gauge rod—a straight-edged timber cut to the planned wall height and marked off in units of 75 mm, the depth of a brick plus a mortar joint—and a mason's line with corner blocks to ensure horizontal alignment when laying courses of bricks *(page 92, Step 1)*. To cut queen closers and any other bricks that may need to be re-sized, use a club hammer and bolster chisel as shown on page 36.

To avoid complications with reinforcement, the height of a freestanding wall should not exceed 1.2 metres. The surface of the concrete footing on which the wall is laid must be absolutely level *(pages 84–89)*. Both the height of the wall and the depth of its footing may be affected by soil conditions and building regulations, so check with your local planning department. If the wall will rise near a property boundary, discuss your plans with your neighbour.

Most brick walls are built 215 mm thick—the length of one header brick laid across the wall, or two stretcher bricks side by side—and are bound together at intervals by header bricks that span the full thickness. In modern bricklaying practice these headers may be replaced by metal wall ties embedded crosswise in the mortar joints of both wall thicknesses. Such walls adapt easily to any decorative treatment based on coloured bricks, on variations in the arrangement of stretchers and headers, or on reliefs created by offsetting bricks. Lattice and serpentine walls, however, are laid in a half-brick thickness, and must be braced at intervals with square brick piers *(pages 99 and 102)*.

A decorative wall, especially one that involves a complex pattern or bricks of varying colours, needs a preliminary sketch of one complete unit of the design. This is essential not only for ordering the bricks but is also helpful later on when setting the bricks. Use graph paper for the sketch, drawing in the individual bricks but increasing their size by 10 mm in every dimension to allow for the mortar joints. Indicate any changes in colour with a coloured pencil.

To estimate the number of bricks required, first multiply the length of the wall (measured in metres) by its height and, for a 215 mm-thick wall, double this figure to give the total surface area. Then multiply this figure by 60, the number of standard-sized bricks in a square metre of wall. Buy 5 per cent more bricks than the estimated amount to allow for breakages. For each square metre of wall surface, you will require 0.05 cubic metres of mortar.

In choosing your bricks, keep in mind that perforated bricks, though they are easier to break and are suitable for most patterned walls, cannot be used for lattice-work or for offset bricks. Solid bricks are also essential for capping walls and piers. Ask for engineering or semi-engineering bricks, which have a high resistance to frost. The dimensions of a single standard-sized brick are 215 by 102.5 by 65 mm.

As you work, set piles of bricks and full boards of mortar at convenient points along the wall, and keep a bucket of clean water or a hose nearby to clean your trowel and spirit level. Wet down the finished wall and keep it moist for several days until the mortar has cured. After a couple of weeks, clean off any areas of efflorescence that may have developed on the bricks with a stiff brush and a damp sponge.

Building the Stopped End of an English Bond Wall

1 **Laying the first bricks.** Snap a chalk line 100 mm from the front edge of a 430 mm-wide concrete footing the planned length of the wall plus 100 mm at each end. Lay a dry run of stretcher bricks along the chalk line, allowing for 10 mm joints between bricks, and mark the ends of the wall to accommodate an exact number of stretchers—this will avoid having to cut bricks for both the wall and its coping *(page 93)*. Mark the joints and remove the dry run. At one end of the planned wall, throw a mortar line the thickness of the wall and about 500 mm long just behind the chalk line. Lay the first header on the mortar bed and check its height against a gauge rod. Also check that the brick is level and plumb. Then lay a queen closer—a brick cut lengthwise to a width of 46 mm—and a further five headers. Adjust all the bricks for level using the first brick as a reference, and make sure they are flush with the chalk line.

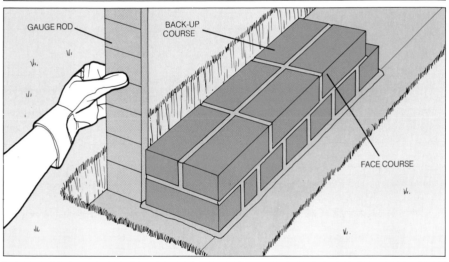

2 **Laying the stretcher course.** Throw a mortar line over the bricks laid in Step 1 and set a stretcher at the end of the wall face. Gauge, level and plumb this brick carefully—it will be used as a reference for levelling later bricks in the course. Lay a further two stretchers on the same line and, behind them, three stretchers in the back-up course. Fill between the two courses with mortar and check that all the stretchers are level and flush with the sides of the header course; check their height with the gauge rod *(left)*. As you work, cut off all excess mortar with a trowel before it dries on the brick face.

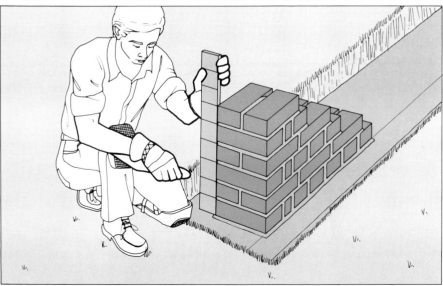

3 **Finishing the first stopped end.** For the third course lay one header, a queen closer and three further headers. The fourth course consists of two stretchers on the face course and two stretchers on the back-up course. The fifth course is a header, a queen closer and one more header; and the final course is two stretchers one behind the other. As each course is laid, check for height, level and plumb.

4 **Building the second stopped end.** At the opposite end of the footing, repeat Steps 1 to 3 to build a matching six-course stopped end. By constantly checking with the gauge rod and level, make sure the new stopped end exactly matches the first one: if they do not match, it may be impossible to level the completed wall, and you may have to start it afresh.

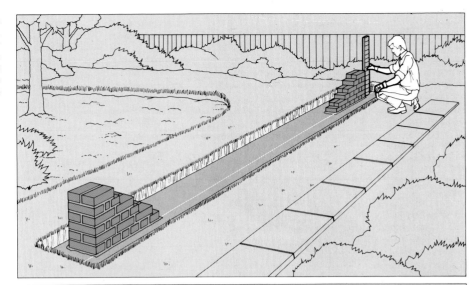

Joining the Stopped Ends

1 **Building between the stopped ends.** Install a mason's line with corner blocks between the stopped ends, aligning the string with the top edges of the first brick course *(top inset)*. Working from the stopped ends towards the centre and using the mason's line as a guide, lay the first course of headers along the footing. Complete the remaining courses to the tops of the stopped ends, alternating header and stretcher courses; move the line as each course is finished.

If the wall is over 6 metres long, support the centre of the mason's line with a tingle plate, a thin metal plate jutting out about 10 mm from the wall and laid on a brick gauged to the correct height *(bottom inset)*. The tingle plate is held in position by a loose brick or a lump of mortar.

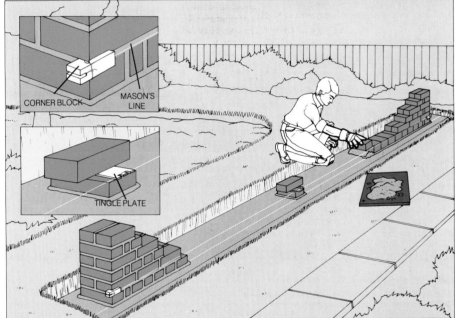

CORNER BLOCK   MASON'S LINE

TINGLE PLATE

2 **Extending the wall upwards.** Lay new stopped ends on top of the wall you have just completed to bring the wall to the desired height, and fill them in as described in Step 1, above. If you wish to add coping bricks on top of the wall in the arrangement shown opposite, finish off the wall with a course of headers.

Finishing a Wall with a Decorative Coping

1 **Laying the coping's first course.** Having completed the English bond wall with a course of headers, lay a dry run for the first course of the coping. Begin with two stretchers laid one behind the other and flush with the end of the wall, followed by three bricks on edge laid crosswise and spaced 10 mm apart. Follow the bricks on edge with two stretchers, then a further three crosswise bricks on edge, and continue this pattern to the other end of the wall. Mark the brick positions on the top of the last header course of the wall, then remove the dry run and throw a two-stretcher-long bed of mortar on one end of the wall. Lay the first stretcher and gauge, level and plumb it. Use this stretcher as a reference for laying the back-up stretcher, then repeat this process at the other end of the wall. Allowing about 15 minutes for the mortar to harden, set up corner blocks and a line to mark the top edge of the stretchers; lay loose stretchers on the mortared stretchers to hold the corner blocks in position. Using the line as a guide, lay all the intermediate bricks as in the dry run, working from the ends of the wall towards the middle. Clean excess mortar from the bricks as you work.

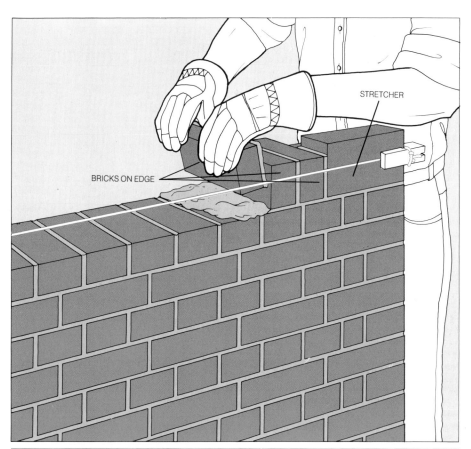

2 **Completing the coping.** Throw a mortar bed over the first stretchers at one end of the wall and set a wrought-iron cramp centrally to the thickness of the wall with its long arm embedded in the mortar and its short arm pointing vertically upwards. Lay the first brick on edge crosswise and adjust the cramp so it is firmly against the side of the brick *(inset)*. Then lay the remaining two crosswise bricks over the stretchers and check for level and plumb. Repeat at the other end of the wall. After allowing the mortar to harden, set up corner blocks and a line and cover the remaining stretchers with crosswise bricks on edge.

Enlivening a Brick Wall with Geometric Designs

Three decorative bonds. In an English bond wall, courses of headers and stretchers are alternated; in Flemish bond, headers and stretchers are alternated in each course. Several variants of Flemish bond create more elaborate geometric patterns, which can be enhanced if different coloured bricks are used. Cross bond *(right)*, for example, alternates standard Flemish courses with courses consisting entirely of stretchers.

Flemish spiral bond *(right, centre)* bands the wall with diagonal lines of contrasting headers. Constructed of standard Flemish courses, the bond is laid so that the headers in successive courses are staggered one-half their width beyond the headers in the course below, with every course staggered in the same direction.

Garden-wall bond *(right, below)* consists of modified Flemish courses, with three stretchers separating successive headers. In this example, a large diamond is created with rows of contrasting bricks centred over a single contrasting header. With each new course, the row of constrasting bricks is lengthened by half a brick for five rows; thereafter each row is shortened by half a brick until, with the ninth course, only a single header remains. For such dovetailing diamond patterns, a preliminary sketch helps you determine the proper placement of the header bricks that form the top, bottom and centre of each diamond.

On brick veneer, where the brickwork will be exposed on only one side, you can accentuate any of these decorative patterns by offsetting the contrasting bricks 12 to 20 mm from the face of the wall, thus creating a pattern in relief.

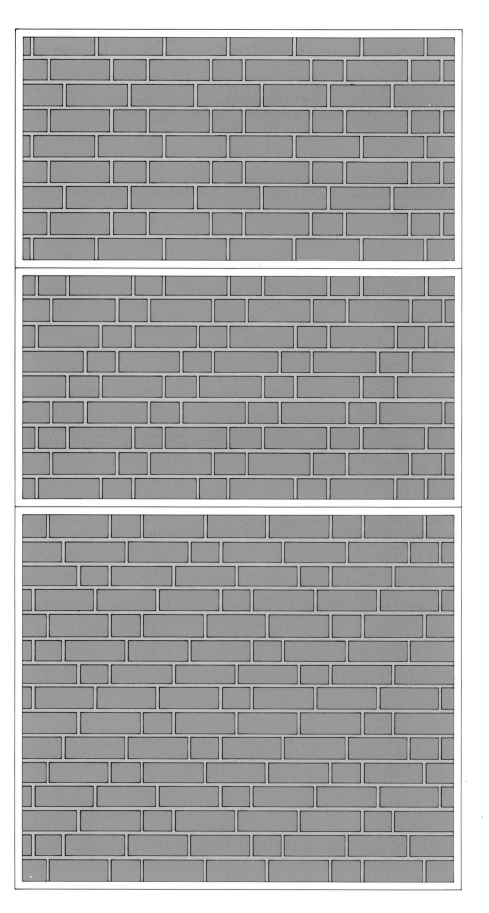

Finishing the Joints

Four ways to shape the mortar. Using a trowel or specially shaped tool, the mortar joints in a wall can be shaped to uniform patterns. In the keyed or concave joint *(right)*, mortar is pressed firmly between the bricks with a convex jointing tool, a dowel, a metal rod or a section of smooth hosepipe; because the mortar is forced tightly into the joints, it makes an excellent bond which readily sheds rainwater. The flush joint *(second from top)* is made by simply trowelling off excess mortar; this is usually done when the mortar has set slightly, but because the mortar is not compacted, it is less water resistant than other joints. The recessed joint *(second from bottom)* is formed by removing up to 5 mm of mortar with a recessing tool or a piece of wood. This joint casts a heavy shadow that accentuates brick courses but is poor at shedding rainwater. Recessed joints are sometimes finished with white or coloured mortar. The weathered joint *(bottom)* is recessed with a trowel up to 5 mm at the top and at an angle which brings it flush with the brick below. This joint has excellent rainwater runoff.

Whichever type of joint you choose, work in an area no larger than 1 square metre at a time, and shape the vertical joints before the horizontal ones. Finishing the joints as the wall is being built is known as "jointing"; if the joints are finished when the wall has been completed, or as part of the restoration of an old wall, the process is called "pointing".

Laying Bricks in Relief

Mortaring an offset brick. On top of the flush course of bricks already laid, throw a mortar line for the offset brick and furrow it very slightly. Set the offset brick in position, then trim away any mortar spilling over the edge of the course below. Check the projection of the offset brick—usually between 12 and 20 mm—with a ruler or piece of scrap timber cut to the required width. Check the brick also for plumb and level, and fill in the space between the offset brick and the back-up course with mortar. Trim the joints with a trowel or joint filler.

A Rusticated Quoin: Relief for the Eye

1 **Laying the first projecting course.** Raise the inner and outer faces of the wall to the same height on both sides of the corner; in the wall shown, a stretcher bond pattern of overlapping stretcher bricks with staggered vertical joints is used. Working only on the outer face, spread a bed of mortar across the vertical mortar joint nearest the corner; continue the line of mortar along the adjacent leg of the wall a distance of two brick lengths. Lay a corner brick, projecting it 20 mm from both faces of the wall; use a piece of wood 20 mm thick as a guide *(below, left)*. Lay a second brick end to end with the first. Check for horizontal alignment with a level, first along the top of the bricks, then along their outer faces, and check both ends of the projecting bricks with the 20 mm gauge. Adjust them, if necessary, by tapping them with a trowel handle.

Lay a third brick at the corner, along the other leg of the wall *(below, right)*. Set it flush with the first brick and check its horizontal alignment, using a level first along the top and then along the outer faces, as above. Check the height of this first offset course with a gauge rod *(page 91)*.

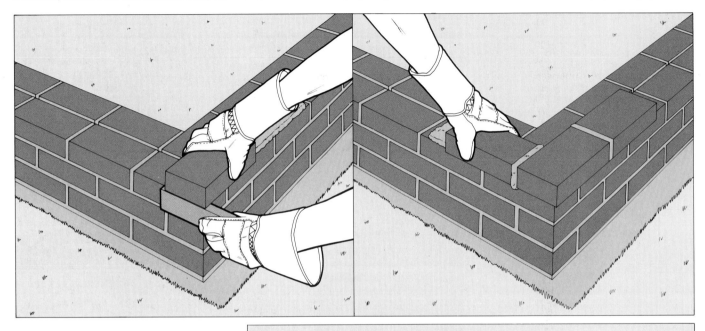

2 **Completing the first course of the corner.** With the first layer of projecting bricks in place, lay 10 mm sections of brick against the projecting bricks and flush with the face of the wall. With their 10 mm mortar joints, the sections will compensate for the quoin's offset and re-establish the stretcher bond pattern exactly. Lay three or four bricks along both legs of the flush course after the brick slivers. Check the first brick with a gauge rod and both legs of this flush course with a level.

To complete the corner, lay bricks along the inner face, flush with the course below.

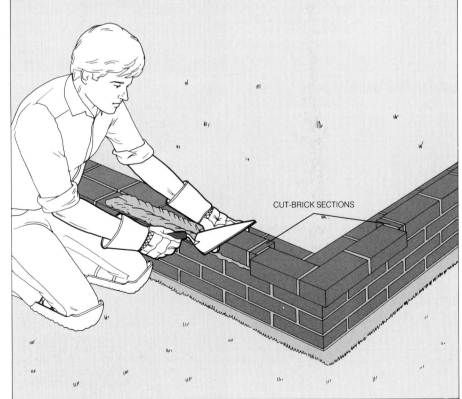

CUT-BRICK SECTIONS

3 **Building up the quoin.** Lay a second course of projecting bricks, using a half-brick at the end of each leg so that the end bricks of the quoin line up with each other. Build the second course of the corner along both legs with bricks set flush with the wall surface. Begin these flush sections with a brick equal in length to a half-brick plus the length of the projection, and end them when the second course is a half-brick short of the first course. Then build the inner row of the second course as in Step 2.

Continue to lay courses of offset bricks until the quoin is the desired height—usually five courses. Follow the patterns of bricks established in the first two courses, and at every second course set metal wall ties across the inner and outer rows to bind them together. At frequent intervals, check the offset and flush bricks for plumb and for horizontal alignment. Align each course with a gauge rod.

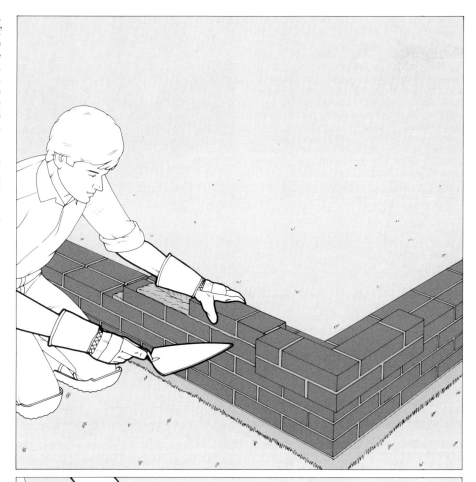

4 **Finishing the quoin.** When the quoin is five courses high, lay a course of bricks flush with the face of the wall. Begin the course with a brick spanning the vertical mortar joint nearest the corner, setting the brick 20 mm in from the faces of the quoin *(right)*. Continue to lay bricks in this course, ending a half-brick short of the previous course. Lay a second course of bricks in the same manner. Then build up the inner thickness of wall to the level of these two courses.

Build either a rusticated quoin or a conventional corner at the opposite end of the wall.

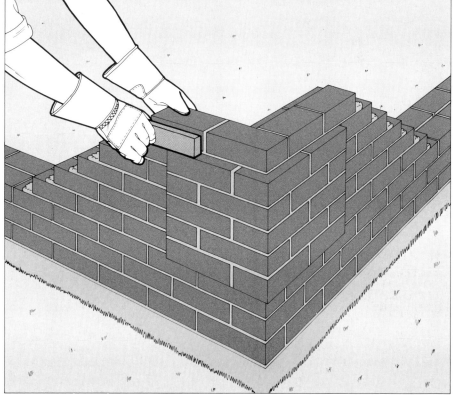

5 **Filling in the wall.** Run a mason's line between the first courses of the corners, anchoring the line near the quoin with a line pin driven into the mortar. Attach the line similarly at the other corner or fasten it to corner blocks fitted around the corners. Adjust the line to run even with the top of the course. Lay bricks in mortar from corner to corner, spacing the bricks evenly. Lay a matching course of bricks along the inner surface of the wall.

Reposition the mason's line along the top of the next course, and continue to raise the wall in this fashion until it is even with the top of the recessed band of the quoin.

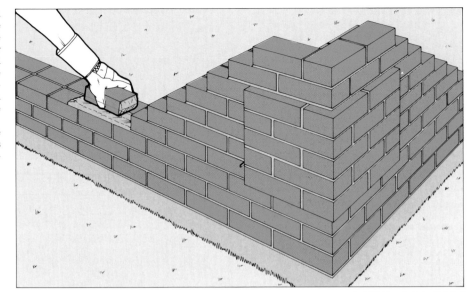

6 **Adding a second quoin.** Lay a course of projecting bricks as in Step 1, beginning with a brick covering the vertical mortar joint nearest the corner. Since this joint now lies on the other leg of the wall, the positions of the long and short legs of the quoin will be reversed. Using the brick pattern set by these two courses, build up the second quoin and its corner as in Steps 2 to 5. Then fill in the intervening wall. Continue building up the wall in this way, alternating rusticated quoins with standard courses.

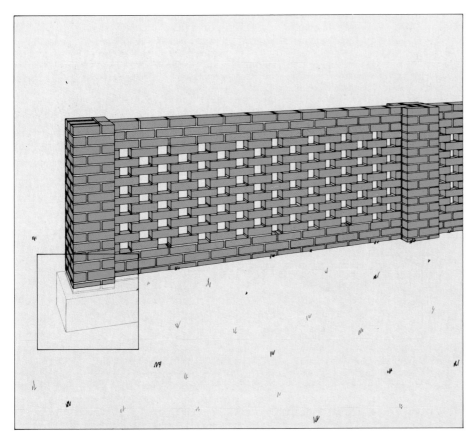

A Brick Screen That Lets Air Circulate

Anatomy of a honeycomb wall. A 6 metre screen, long enough to add privacy to a patio or to conceal a carport, consists of two long openwork brick panels buttressed by three brick piers. The panels, just the width of a half-brick, are banded top and bottom by three courses of solid brickwork to frame the honeycomb and add stability. The honeycomb bricks are spaced to leave open pockets. With 11 courses of honeycomb and six courses of solid brickwork, the wall is about 1.2 metres high.

Like all brick walls, the screen rests on a concrete footing. In this example, the concrete slab is 250 mm thick and the top of the slab is 50 mm below ground level. The slab is 450 mm wide, which allows for 50 mm of clearance on either side of the piers, and it projects 50 mm beyond the ends of the brickwork. In many areas, a footing of this design is adequate only for lightweight walls; because of this, and because honeycomb brickwork is fragile, you should limit your screen to the height shown.

Building a Honeycomb Wall

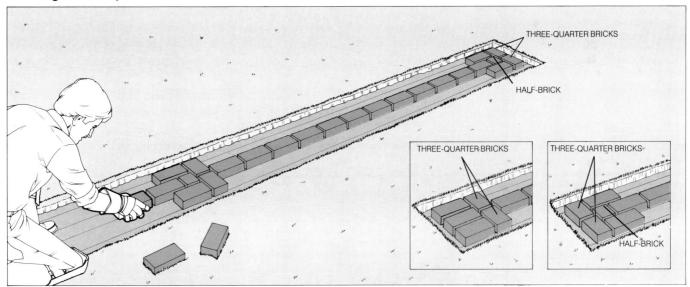

THREE-QUARTER BRICKS

HALF-BRICK

THREE-QUARTER BRICKS

THREE-QUARTER BRICKS

HALF-BRICK

1 A dry run. Snap two chalk lines equidistant from the centre of the slab and 327 mm apart to mark the outer faces of the piers. Snap a second pair of lines, 102 mm apart and 112 mm in from the pier lines, to mark the outer faces of the panels. Measure off and mark where the piers will cross these lines and lay bricks in a dry run for the bottom course. Begin with an end pier, following the arrangement shown above, so that the first brick of the wall panel intersects the pier. Then lay bricks to the middle pier, spacing the mortar joints so that the last brick falls a mortar joint away from the pier mark or half way across the pier mark. Lay out the second pier, reversing or using the same arrangement as for the first pier, then repeat the procedure for the second panel and the third pier, which should match one of the layouts shown in the insets.

2 **A band of solid brickwork.** Lay the first course of each pier in mortar, as well as the first two bricks at each end of the panels. Check the mortar bed for thickness with a gauge rod, and check the horizontal alignment of the bricks with a level. Lay two more courses on the piers and the panels, alternating the arrangement of bricks on the pier so that the first bricks of the panels step back by a half-brick on each course *(below, left)*. Check your work frequently for alignment, plumb and course level.

Drive line pins or nails into the first mortar joints of the panels, and stretch a mason's line between them. Adjust the line to lie flush with the top of the first course of bricks. Use the line as a guide to fill in the intermediate bricks, removing three or four dry-run bricks at a time and replacing them in mortar *(below, right)*. Lay the next two courses, then repeat the process for the second panel. Patch the holes left by the line pins with fresh mortar.

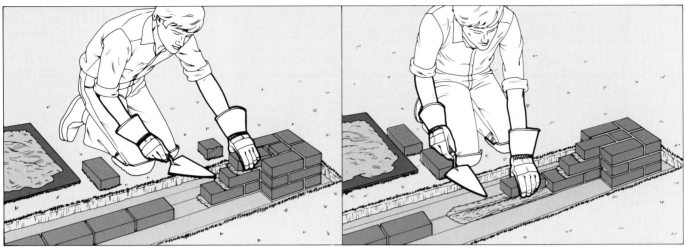

3 **Starting the honeycombing.** Do a dry run of the fourth course, beginning with the pier bricks. Where the pier is intersected by a panel brick, the intersecting brick must be cut by 56 mm before the rest of the course is laid. The resulting three-quarter brick is then set into the pier *(inset)*. Working from the two piers towards the centre, fill in the panel bricks, leaving a space of about 112 mm between them; use the combined width of a header brick and a finger as a convenient space guide. When all the bricks are in place, check to make sure the spacing is even.

Set the pier bricks in mortar. Then remove and set the first three or four bricks at each end of the panel. Use a mortar bed only as long as the brick and carefully remove any excess mortar with a trowel. Check this openwork with a gauge rod and level.

4 **Building honeycombed ends.** Build up the two openwork ends with a second course of pier and panel bricks, positioning the latter to span the 112 mm gaps in the first openwork course. Fix these bricks in place with small beds of mortar placed on the ends of the bricks below. Repeat the process until the openwork ends are five courses high; tie them into the piers as necessary with three-quarter bricks. As you go, check the wall frequently for level and for plumb with a level and a gauge rod.

5 **Filling in the honeycombing.** Stretch a mason's line flush with the top of the first course of the openwork and use it as a guide to set the remaining bricks of that course. Raise the line to match the second course and fill in the second course of openwork, spanning the 112 mm gaps in the first. Continue to fill in the openwork until it is even with the tops of the piers, raising the mason's line with each new course. Patch the holes left by the line pins with fresh mortar. Then repeat the process to raise the second openwork panel to the same height.

To continue building upwards, lay six-course ends as shown in Step 4, then add six courses of openwork. Use a jointing tool to trim away any mortar that has squeezed into the open spaces, leaving a flush finish *(inset)*.

6 **Capping the screen.** Lay a dry run of a new course of solid brickwork along the top of the panels. Adjust the spacing of the mortar joints so that they are even, then build three courses of solid brickwork as in Step 2. Take care not to spill the mortar into the open spaces of the honeycombing as you lay mortar for the first course. Check frequently for plumb and level, and use a gauge rod to make sure the three courses are of uniform thickness. Using a mason's line as guide, fill in the solid brickwork between the ends.

A Wall with Serpentine Grace

Unlike the corrupting serpent in the biblical Garden of Eden, a serpent-shaped, or serpentine, garden wall, meandering among flower beds and casting sinuous shadows, adds only grace and charm to its surroundings. Such a wall, however, presents unusual complexities of design and construction. Classical serpentine walls are built to a thickness of only half a brick. Repeated S-curves, rather than frequent piers and a full thickness of bricks, give these walls stability.

The S-curves of a serpentine wall are a succession of arcs, each an identical segment from a circle of a given radius. The arcs are linked end to end in mirror image down the length of the wall; the size of the arcs determines the wall's inherent strength. The radius of the arcs should be no greater than twice the height of the wall, and the total sweep of the arcs from side to side should cover a distance equal to at least half the height of the wall.

Other design features will increase the strength of a serpentine wall. Although you can have any number of S-curves and can end the wall at any point along a curve, you ought to buttress the ends of the wall with square piers that are at least one and a half bricks thick. For additional reinforcement, set corrugated-steel wall ties after every fifth course, running the ties lengthwise from brick to brick.

As with any wall, a solid footing is essential. For serpentine walls up to 1.2 metres high—a sensible maximum—a concrete footing 250 mm deep and set with its base 300 to 400 mm below ground level should be adequate. Ordinarily, you can simply dig a serpentine trench twice as wide as the wall is thick, then pour the concrete using the sides of the trench themselves as forms. In sandy soil, you may have to dig a wider trench and set up curved forms *(page 87)* to contain the concrete. In clay or in boggy ground, it may be necessary to excavate below the frost line; consult your local planning department about the soil conditions in your area.

Use standard bricklaying techniques to build your wall: lay buttered bricks in a furrowed bed of mortar, and make sure that the vertical mortar joints in successive courses of bricks are staggered. Since the curves of the wall will make it impossible for you to use the conventional stopped ends and mason's line to align the courses, you will have to employ different methods of checking them for plumb, level and curve alignment.

A plywood template spanning two half-arcs, centre point to centre point, is used both when setting out the face line for the first course of bricks on the footing and for checking the alignment of each course as it is laid as shown on page 105, Step 2. If the top of the footing is more than one brick course below ground level, nail to the curved edge of the template a strip of plywood which is twice the depth of the top of the footing below ground—this will enable you to check the alignment of bricks laid below ground level.

The reference line for the template is a string stretched between two poles, one at either end of the wall. As each course is laid, the string is raised accordingly. Use a gauge rod to check the height of the courses *(page 91, Step 2)*, and a spirit level and straightedge to check that they are plumb and level.

Anatomy of a serpentine wall. This traditional serpentine wall built a half-brick thick rises to a height of just over 1 metre. Each of its undulating curves is a segment of a circle with a radius of 1800 mm. On either side of the wall, the distance between the outermost points of successive curves is approximately 900 mm. Brick piers buttress the ends of the wall, and corrugated-steel wall ties running from brick to brick after every fifth course provide additional strength.

Below ground level, the wall rests on a similarly curved concrete footing which is 450 mm wide, 250 mm deep and 100 mm longer than the wall at each end. The top of the footing is 50 mm below ground level.

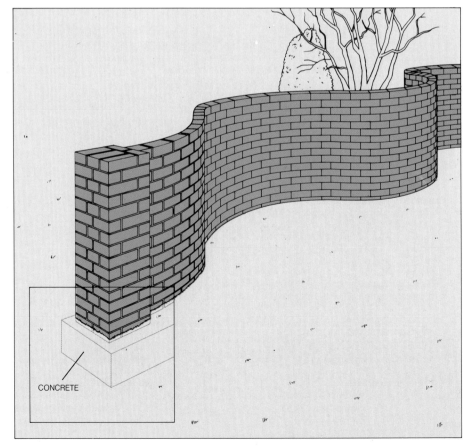

CONCRETE

Laying the Groundwork for the Wall

1 Tracing the template. Rule a parallel base line 30 mm in from one of the long edges of a 2440 by 1220 mm sheet of 12 mm plywood. Attach one end of a length of picture wire to a stake or other fixed object. Measure out 1800 mm along the wire from the stake, which becomes the centre point, and twist the wire around a felt-tipped marker. Position the plywood so that the marker wire, stretched along one end of the plywood, extends 900 mm past the base line *(inset)*. With the wire taut, draw an arc across the plywood.

Reverse the plywood and adjust the sheet so that the wire runs parallel to the other end, 30 mm in from the edge, with the marker ex-tending just to the base line. Draw an arc towards the centre of the sheet, extending the curve until the two arcs touch. With a jigsaw, cut along the marked lines to free the template from the waste *(inset)*, starting at the end of one arc and switching to the other arc at the point where the two touch each other.

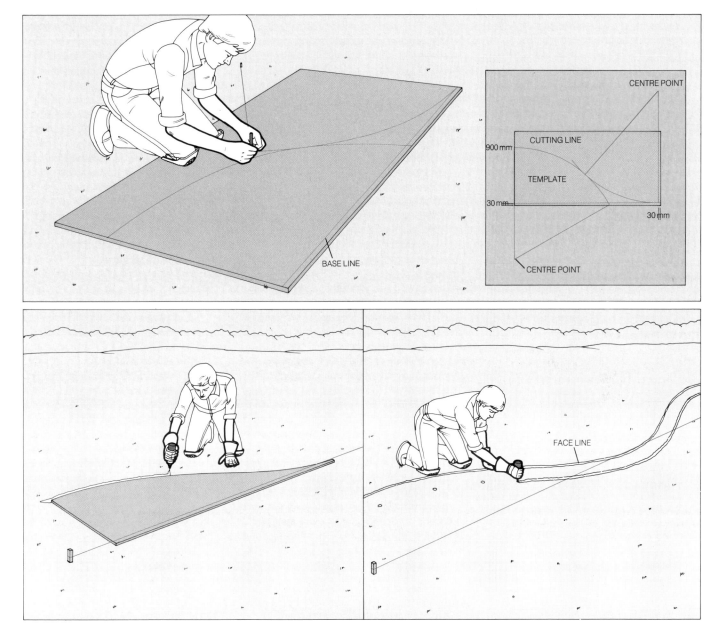

2 Outlining the footing trench. Stretch a reference string along a line representing the outermost curves of the face of the wall. Make the string slightly longer than the planned wall and secure it to two stakes so that it lies about 25 mm above the ground. Position the template near one end of the string, with the ruled base line directly under the string *(above, left)*. Outline the curved edge of the template with chalk. Then turn the template end over end and mark off the desired number of serpentine curves. Mark a series of reference points 175 mm out from the face line, and join the points with chalk to outline parallel serpen-tine curves *(above, right)*. On the other side of the face line, draw another parallel line of serpentine curves following the same method but at a dis-tance of 275 mm from the face line. Extend the curved lines at each end with straight, parallel lines about 450 mm long to mark the footings for the piers.

Remove the reference string, dig a footing trench between the outer chalk lines and pour a footing *(pages 86–89)*. Allow it to cure for 48 hours before starting to lay bricks for the wall.

3 **Setting the reference line.** Mark the outermost curves for the face of the wall by re-establishing the reference string between poles at least as high as the planned wall. Make sure these poles are vertical and driven firmly into the ground. Mark the course heights on one of the poles, starting from the top of the footing. Repeat for the other pole, using a water level to align the lowest mark with its equivalent on the first pole.

Outline the face line of the wall on the footing, using the template. Place the base line directly under the string—which should be set at the height of the first course—and draw a crayon line along the curved edge, turning the template end over end, as in Step 2; allow 450 mm at each end of the footing for piers. Use a steel square to trace an outline for each pier, leaving a 60 mm margin at the sides and 120 mm at the end.

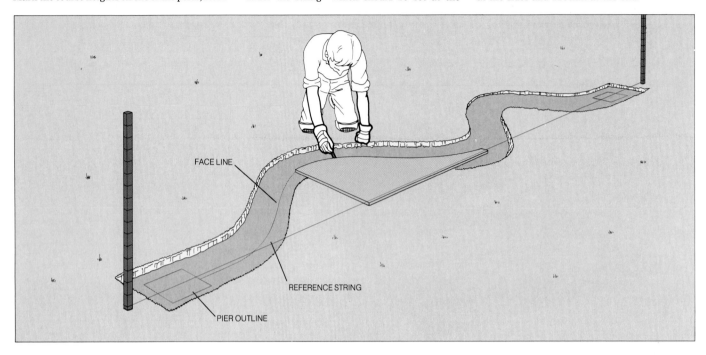

FACE LINE

REFERENCE STRING

PIER OUTLINE

Raising the Wall

1 **Laying a dry run.** Lay a dry course of bricks inside one pier outline; then lay a course of bricks down the centre of the footing, aligning them with the crayon line that marks the face of the wall. To allow for mortar joints, space the bricks so that the gap at the centre of the joints is about 10 mm. When you reach the opposite pier outline, adjust the spacing between the last few bricks so that the final brick either falls a mortar joint short of the outline or overlaps the outline at the brick's midpoint. Then lay a dry course of bricks for the pier, if necessary using cut bricks to interlock properly with the wall *(page 99)*. Mark the positions of the apex bricks—the bricks at the outermost points of the curves—on the footing.

2 **Checking alignment.** Set the apex bricks in mortar, using a spirit level taped to a length of straight timber to check that the apex bricks on the string side of the face line are at the same level as those on the other side. Then, starting at a pier, lay the intermediate bricks along the face line in a four-step sequence: remove three or four bricks from the dry run at a time, throw and furrow a line of mortar, butter the bricks and place them back in position. As you complete each sequence, check for course level by spanning to the nearest apex brick with the timber-mounted spirit level *(below, left)*. At each pier, check that the inner points are level with the nearest apex brick, and that the outer points are level with the inner points. To lower a brick, tap it with a trowel handle; to raise one, take it up and re-lay it using more mortar. Once a section of wall between a pier and an apex brick, or between one apex brick and the next, is completed, have a helper set the template into the curve, and look down on it from above. If a brick is not aligned, tap it with the trowel handle until it lies against the template's curved edge *(below, right)*.

3 **Adding to the brickwork.** Raise the reference string to the next mark on the poles and continue raising the wall, course by course, resetting the reference string between the poles for each course. Lay the apex bricks first and check them carefully for plumb, level and height; when laying the intermediate bricks, make sure that the vertical joints of the bricks in each course are at the midpoint of the bricks in the course below. As the wall rises, have a pair of helpers hold the template in place while you check the curvature.

After every fifth course, set a steel wall tie across each vertical joint before you throw the mortar for the next course.

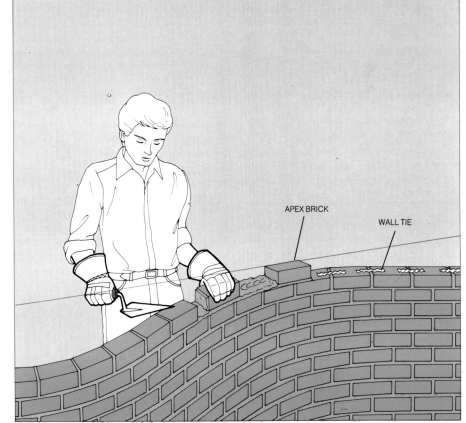

APEX BRICK

WALL TIE

Selecting and Shaping Stone to Meet Your Needs

Stone, as a building material, has a lot to recommend it. The existence of stone buildings many centuries old attests to its strength and durability. Less evident is the fact that the cutting and shaping of stone are relatively simple tasks. Only a few hand tools are needed to be able to fashion this widely available raw material into building blocks and to dress the surfaces to a smooth finish.

Though stone used for construction displays a vast array of colours and textures, most of it falls into half a dozen major types *(chart, opposite page)*. In choosing among them, two factors are paramount: structural strength and workability. A coarse-grained sandstone will crumble, for instance, if it is used for a load-bearing pier or in a wet, exposed location. Dense granite and limestone are suitably sturdy for almost any application, but they can be difficult to split. In fact, if you are planning to cut a great deal of stone into thin slabs for paving or veneer, look for stone that is marked by parallel striations, called the grain; these are natural break lines that will make splitting easier.

Quarried stone, which has been cut or blasted from bedrock, has a fresh-cut appearance and sharper edges. Because it usually retains much of its ground water content, called quarry sap, it is also much easier to cut and shape and its clean, unweathered surface bonds well with mortar. Quarried stone is available in a wide range of shapes and sizes, from fine gravel to individual pieces weighing over 100 kilograms. In construction sizes, most kinds of stone are available either as flat pieces or as irregularly shaped rubble. Flat stones up to 100 mm thick are used for veneering, paving and laying coursed walls. In diameters from 150 to 300 mm, rubble is used for hearths, piers and both mortared and unmortared walls, called "dry" walls.

Beyond the immediate concerns for strength and workability, your choice of stone is likely to be governed by cost. Stone available through building-materials suppliers and garden centres, as well as the marble and polished granite sold by monumental masons, is often brought from distant sources. This adds appreciably to its cost. Because of its great weight, stone is expensive to transport. For this reason, local stone is generally cheaper. In addition, it tends to blend more harmoniously into its surroundings.

If one type of building stone is unusually prevalent in an area, the chances are that a nearby quarry is supplying it. Most quarries will deliver stone directly to the building site, selling it by the square metre if it is flat stone and by the cubic metre or by weight if it is rubble. You can cut costs substantially by hauling the stone yourself in a hired truck or trailer. Some quarries will allow you to select the stone, enabling you to reject unsuitable sizes and shapes.

Even hand-picked stones, however, are unlikely to fit perfectly into every space in your project. And some projects require specially shaped stones such as square-cut pieces, called quoins, for corners, or angled keystones for arches. These can be cut from larger stones and dressed to the desired shape. For jobs requiring paving or veneering, it will be necessary to split thick flat stones into thinner pieces.

Shaping stone is above all a gradual process: impatience can reduce a usable stone to worthless scrap. Study each stone to determine its grain, evidenced by parallel layers or cracks, and plan to capitalize on this direction of natural splitting. Cutting across the grain is more difficult; except where cross-grain cracks are already present, you may get unwanted breaks. If the stone has no natural grain, its cutting characteristics will be the same in any di-

rection, affected only by the density of the stone. In general, a dense stone such as granite requires many chipping blows before an irregular block is turned into a square quoin; far fewer blows are needed to achieve a similar shape in slate or in sandstone, which are less dense.

The mason's basic shaping tool is a special hammer with a head that is blunt at one end and wedge-shaped at the other. Available in sizes ranging from 1 to 4 kilograms (the best weight for general use is 2 kilograms), the stone hammer is used for breaking and splitting large stones or for chipping edges. The club hammer is blunt at both ends. It is used to strike chisels in dressing the face of a stone and to drive the wedge-shaped end of the stone hammer into stubborn splits. A 2 kilogram club hammer will handle most jobs. Also useful for fine shaping of soft stones is a bricklayer's hammer with a chipping blade.

A basic set of chisels to use with the club hammer should include a bolster—a wide-bladed chisel—for splitting, cutting and notching stone; a sharp-tipped pointed chisel called a spike for fine dressing; and several widths of cold chisels, for shearing off small protrusions.

Small stones can be hand-held during the shaping process, but heavier pieces should be placed on a low, sturdy workbench or on the ground. The bench or ground should be cushioned with rubber pads, sand, sawdust or several layers of carpet to absorb the force of the cutting blow. Lack of cushioning may cause the stone to break at the point where it touches the work surface rather than on the face that is being struck.

Finally, whenever you cut or dress stone, wear leather gloves and protective goggles to guard against injury from jagged edges and flying shards. Kneepads will make kneeling more comfortable.

A Guide to Common Building Stones

Type	Weight	Durability	Water resistance	Workability	Colour	Texture	Uses
Granite	Heavy	Good	Good	Difficult	Various greys	Fine to coarse	Building
Basalt	Heavy	Excellent	Excellent	Difficult	Black	Fine	Paving
Limestone	Heavy	Fair	Poor	Medium to difficult	Various	Fine to coarse	Building, veneering
Slate	Medium	Good	Excellent	Easy	Purple, grey, green	Fine	Veneering, paving
Shale	Medium	Poor	Poor	Easy	Various	Fine	Veneering
Sandstone	Light to medium	Fair	Fair	Easy to medium	Various	Fine to coarse	Building, veneering

Choosing stone. This chart shows the relative weights and other properties of the basic stone types used in construction. It is only a general guide; stones in each type can vary greatly, depending on the region where they are found.

Splitting a Stone into Flat Slabs

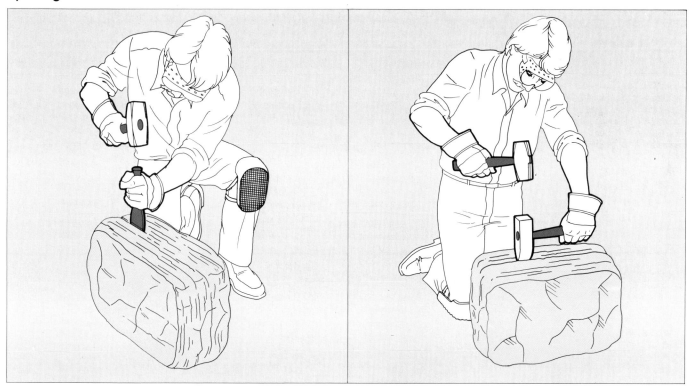

Chiselling with the grain. Incise the splitting line on one long face of the stone with a bolster, tapping the bolster lightly with a club hammer *(above, left)*. When you have marked the entire line, return to the starting point and strike the bolster with more force, working along the line once again. Repeat until the stone splits. If the stone cracks but does not split, you will have to use a stone hammer: align its wedge-shaped end with the crack *(above, right),* then strike the flat face of the hammer firmly with the club hammer. Move the stone hammer little by little along the crack you have made, striking it repeatedly until the stone splits apart.

Squaring the Faces of a Corner Stone

1 Rough-chipping a flat face. Scribe the cutting line on the stone with the corner of a bolster and lay the stone on the ground, waste edge facing you. Chip off small pieces from the waste edge by striking the stone glancing blows with the blunt end of the stone hammer; hold the hammer at a slight angle so that only the edge of the hammer face strikes the stone. Continue chipping until you have reduced most of the surface unevenness and are within 12 mm of the cutting line. Check your work occasionally with a square to make sure that the new face is perpendicular to the adjoining faces of the stone.

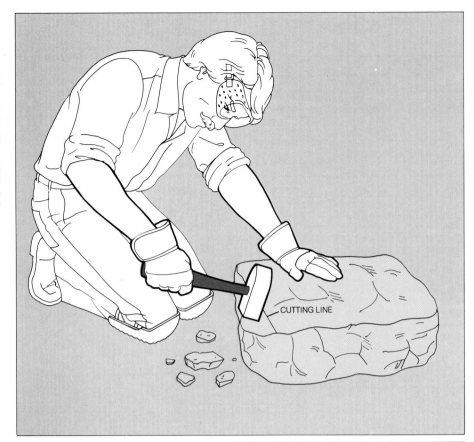

2 Dressing the flattened face. Turn the stone on end and, using a 25 mm chisel with a 2 kilogram club hammer, chisel away the remaining waste edge. Hold the chisel at about a 30-degree angle to the face of the stone and work from the ends towards the centre, cutting a little at a time and turning the stone as required. When only small protrusions remain, remove them with a spike, using the same chiselling technique.

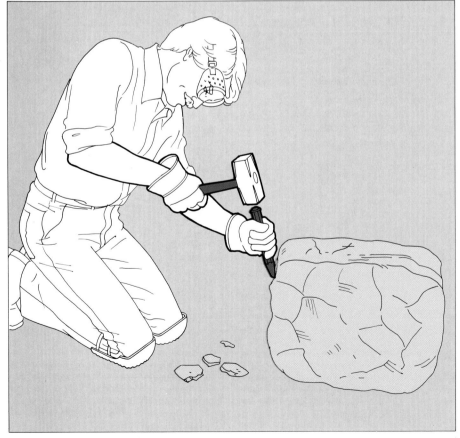

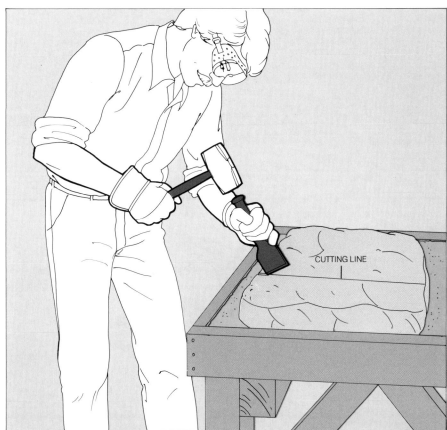

CUTTING LINE

Breaking Across a Stone's Grain

1 Cutting a groove. Working on the ground or on a cushioned workbench, cut a shallow groove across one face of the stone with a bolster and a club hammer. Hold the bolster so that only a corner of its blade comes into contact with the stone, and tap it lightly. Repeat this cut, each time tapping the bolster more firmly, until the depth of the groove is about one-fifth of the stone's thickness. Turn the stone over and groove the other face in the same way, lining up the grooves as accurately as possible. Then groove each edge so that the stone is completely girdled.

2 Snapping off the waste. Align the groove with the edge of the workbench or a sturdy board, and strike the overhanging waste edge with a stone hammer. Bring the hammer down sharply, full face against the surface of the stone. If necessary, press down on the other edge of the stone with your free hand so that the stone will not flip up from the force of the blow.

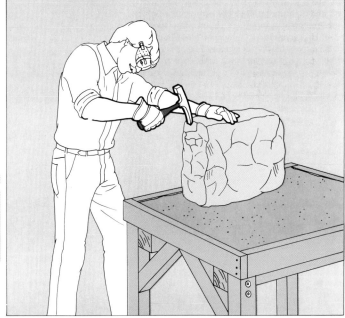

3 Dressing the cut edge. Stand the stone upright, cut edge facing you, and chip away small uneven parts with the chisel end of a bricklayer's hammer. Work towards the centre of the stone and strike across the base of each protrusion, in effect lifting it from the surface of the stone. To remove any large protrusions, use a chisel and a club hammer as shown opposite, Step 2.

Chipping Stone into a Curve

1 **Scoring the curve.** Make a template of heavy cardboard cut to the desired curve and, using it as a guide, scratch a cutting line on the face of the stone with the corner of a bolster. Mark the opposite face of the stone in the same manner, aligning the template with the first cutting line at the edges of the stone. Then score grooves along both of these lines, using a bolster and a club hammer, as described on page 109, Step 1.

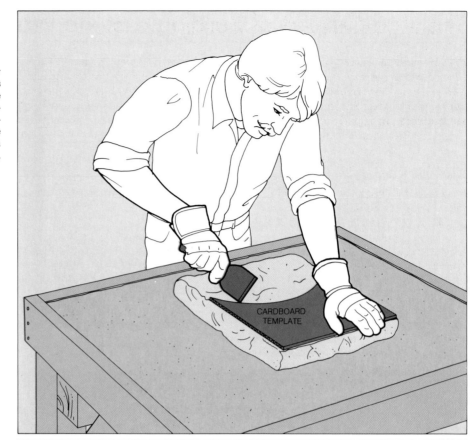

2 **Removing the waste.** Working along the edge of the waste, chip out large flakes, about half the thickness of the stone, using the chisel end of a bricklayer's hammer. When the entire edge has been undercut, or thinned, tap the flat side of the edge with a stone hammer to snap it off. Then undercut the new edge of the waste in the same way, continuing to remove the stone in flakes until you reach the scored groove defining the curve. Then dress, or finish, the curved edge with a chisel and a spike *(page 108, Step 2)*.

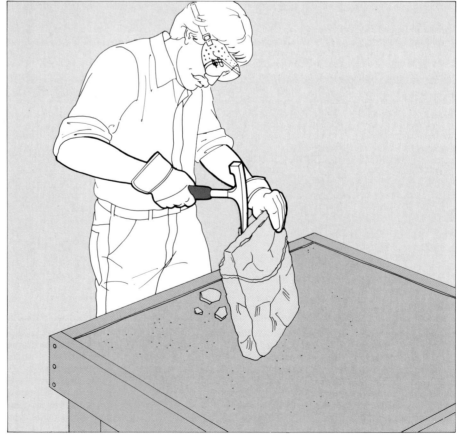

The Age-Old Art of Building a Stone Wall

Stonemasonry is based on the principle that no two stones have exactly the same shape. Unlike factory-made bricks and blocks, which fit together in neat rectangular patterns, irregularly shaped stones form a random mosaic that can never be duplicated. The unique shapes of stones account for much of stonework's beauty but they also pose its greatest problem: when stones are being laid, every one needs a firm support on which to rest.

The bottom course in any stone wall—whether freestanding *(below)* or veneer *(page 112, above)*—must be supported by a sturdy footing *(page 84)*. The stones lying on the footing must be bedded solidly in the mortar to stop them shifting or slipping on the flat surface of the concrete slab.

Because the stones' weight would force mortar of normal consistency out of the joints, use a much stiffer mixture for stonemasonry than for bricks or blocks.

Combine 1 part Portland cement to 3 parts sand for hard stone such as granite and 1 part Portland cement to up to 7 parts sand for the softest stone. But add only enough water—usually about 20 per cent less than normal—to make a mixture that can be squeezed into a compact ball.

When you are ready to begin work, sort through your stones and save the obvious corner pieces: the larger ones with two flat faces that meet in a neat 90-degree angle or that can easily be squared by cutting *(page 108)*. Also make a mental note of the proportion of roughly rectangular stones to those without any particular shape, and the proportion of large stones to small ones. As you build up the wall, use stones in the same proportions, regularly incorporating different sizes and shapes for a balanced appearance.

When laying stones, proceed slowly and deliberately, respecting each piece for the aesthetic and structural opportunities it presents. Trowel a bed of mortar for each stone to rest on. Position stones on the wall so that their top surfaces are level or slope down towards the core. The mortar joints may weaken over time, but the pull of gravity will help keep the stones in place.

Keep the first course of stones in alignment by sighting along guide strings attached to profile boards *(page 85)*. Then switch to a mason's line stretched between nails or line pins pegged in the mortar joints. As you work, always try to place a large, heavy stone over two or three smaller ones to spread and balance its weight. And, to prevent vertical rifts in the wall, avoid aligning vertical joints from course to course.

And be patient: an experienced bricklayer can lay 20 square metres of concrete block a day, but a master stonemason averages only 5 square metres of stonework.

Two Ways to Use Stone: Solid and Veneer

A double-thick stone wall. A stone garden wall consisting of two faces of large and small stones sits squarely upon a wide, sturdy poured-concrete footing. Joining the footing and the first course, which consists of large blocks that fit together easily, is a thick bed of mortar. Stones in the remaining courses are mixed, large and small. Irregular stones, called chinking stones, fill large gaps between stones. Stone chips and mortar fill the core between the two faces of the wall. Traversing the core every 300 mm are long tie stones which, like header bricks *(page 90)*, bond together the two wall faces. For extra strength, vertical mortar joints are staggered from course to course. A 65 mm-thick flagstone coping, mortared in place, provides a weatherproof cap.

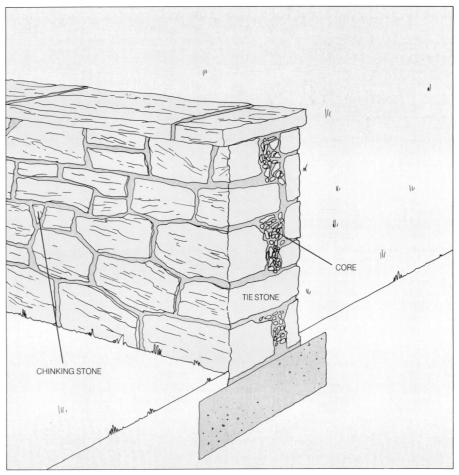

CORE

TIE STONE

CHINKING STONE

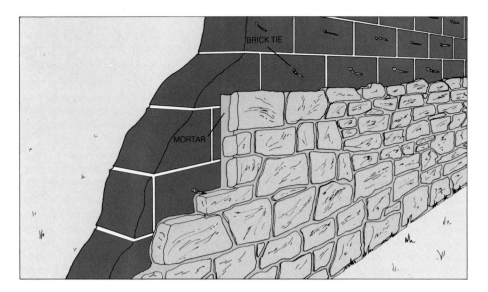

A stone-veneer wall. A single thickness of stone, self-supporting but essentially decorative, rests on the same footing as the concrete-block wall that it covers. The pattern of the stone reflects the masonry principles used to erect freestanding walls—although a veneer wall does not support a structure, it must support itself. Stones are set firmly in position, with mortar at their backs as well as above and below. Strengthening the mortar bond between the block wall and the stone veneer are bendable stainless-steel brick ties screwed into each block.

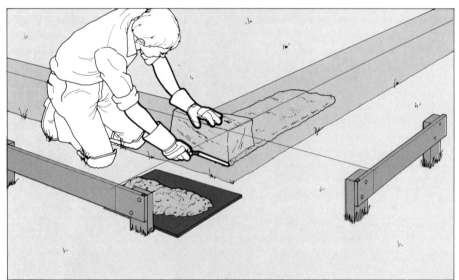

Mortaring the First Course

1 **Setting the corner stones.** Spread a mortar bed 25 mm thick on the footing, aligning it with strings previously stretched between the guide lines marked on the profile boards. Lay the corner stone on the mortar, aligning it too with the guide strings. With a joint filler, force more mortar between the footing and the stone until the two corner faces of the stone are plumb. Go on with the first course, using large stones that fit together easily; leave a 15 mm gap between stones. At every corner, use a corner stone.

If, after setting a stone, you decide to move it, lift it out and wash it thoroughly to remove unwanted mortar. When the first course is completed, take away the guide line strings and allow the mortar to dry.

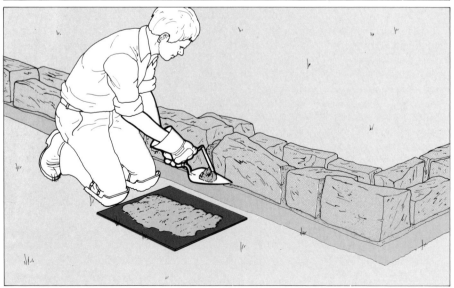

2 **Filling vertical joints.** Scoop up mortar on a trowel and, using the trowel as a palette, pack mortar into the vertical gaps between stones with a joint filler. Fill the joints until the stones are firmly wedged together; do not push in too much mortar or you will force the stones out of position. If mortar begins to ooze out of a joint, catch it with the point of the trowel and dump it into the core of the wall.

3 **Building up the core.** After laying the first course, drop small stones and shards into the core between the two thicknesses, and bond the chips and scraps together with additional mortar thinned to a consistency that makes it easy to work round the stones. When the core is filled level with the top of the first course, trowel on a new mortar bed but do not smooth it; leave it loose enough to conform to the bottom surfaces of the next course of stones. Lay corner stones at both ends of the next course; alternate short and long sides of the corner stones to make strong corners. Then, at the corners of the wall, insert nails or line pins in the mortar joints and string a mason's line *(page 92)*. The line will help you keep the face of the wall plumb as you work.

After laying each course, fill and level the core. Then lay corner stones for the next course and move the mason's line up to the next level. Cap the wall with 65 mm slabs of flagstone; these will keep it weathertight.

Finally, cover the footing with topsoil to make it flush with the surrounding ground. If you are replacing turf, tamp the soil before laying it.

Balancing Stones with Irregular Shapes

Chinking large gaps. If a large gap occurs between two stones, use a bricklayer's hammer to tap a small stone—a chinking stone—into the unsightly joint. Choose a chinking stone that improves the wall's appearance and helps level the top of the course to receive the stone above.

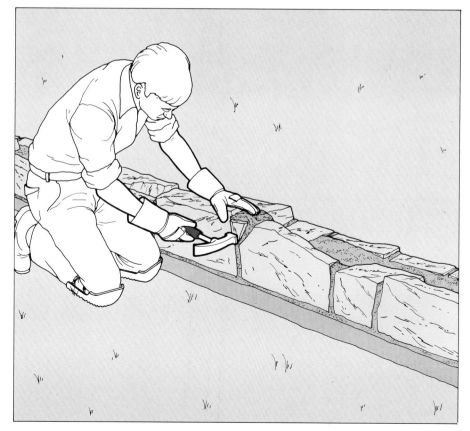

Shimming and shoring stones. If the irregular bottom of a stone makes it wobble, wedge a V-shaped stone chip—called a shim—into the mortar underneath the stone *(below, left.* Leave the shim in place to steady the stone and keep it aligned while the mortar is setting. Then chisel out the shim and fill the hole with fresh mortar.

For a teetering stone that is too large to be steadied with a stone shim, use a 100 by 50 mm board as a diagonal brace instead. Position the length of 100 by 50 at the correct angle to support the stone, then anchor the board at ground level with a heavy stone *(below, right).* When the mortar has set, remove the wooden brace.

Dressing mortar joints. After the mortar in each joint has been allowed to set for 30 to 45 minutes, offset the stones by using a pointing trowel to recess the joints no deeper than 12 mm. Then use a stiff-bristled brush, such as an old paintbrush, to smooth the remaining mortar.

Understanding the Principles of the Brick Arch

The structural purpose of an arch is to span an opening and support the weight of the masonry above it. In a brick arch, mortar holds the bricks together but gravity is what actually holds them in place. Either the mortar joints or the bricks themselves have to be slightly wedge-shaped so that the weight of the load upon the wedges forces the bricks in the arch tightly together. The arch then conveys its load on to the supporting walls.

Arches have been a popular architectural feature for many centuries, but in modern brickwork or masonry they are more often built for the beauty of their form than for their structural advantages. In brick veneer, for example, an arch supports only a small section of bricks directly above it. Whatever its purpose, the arch must be properly proportioned and carefully built in order to last.

Segmental and semicircular arches *(below and page 116, above)*, both commonly used in garden walls and to span the openings for doors and windows, are the simplest types of arch to design. Construction techniques for the semicircular arch are shown on the following pages. Elliptical and pointed arches can be built using the same techniques, but their design and structural planning will require professional expertise.

Although an arch may not serve a larger structural purpose, it does have to be self-supporting. Consequently, any arch, regardless of its shape, should have a face height at least as great as the thickness of the wall surrounding it, and its depth should equal the thickness of the wall. Structural considerations also limit the distance an arch can safely span. Do not undertake to build an arch more than 1.5 metres wide. Although an arch can span a distance greater than this, such a project should be left to an experienced bricklayer.

All arches are constructed with the aid of a temporary support called the centre. For brick arches, the centre can be built with 12 mm plywood and 100 by 50 mm pieces of timber. The centre serves as a template while the bricks are being laid and carries the load of the arch until the mortar sets. The centre should stay in place for about a week after the arch is completed.

There are two general methods of building brick arches. One method is to use standard bricks and shape the mortar joints; the alternative is to use specially shaped bricks so that the joints can be uniform. Shaped bricks, custom-made at the factory to your specifications, are available in sets from brick manufacturers; bricks can also be custom-cut by brick-cutting specialists. Such bricks generally produce a better-looking arch, but they are more expensive. Alternatively, you can cut the bricks yourself *(page 36)*.

If you do choose to order factory-shaped or custom-cut bricks, supply a full-sized drawing of the arch: include full specifications for the rise and span of the arch, its face height and the number of rings. Also, plan the project well in advance because delivery of the bricks is likely to be slow, probably about three months. A full-sized drawing is a useful idea in any event, since it eliminates mistakes in planning and facilitates construction of the centre.

Before starting on an arch, build corners or stopped ends *(page 92)* for the surrounding masonry to the finished height of the arch. These should be far enough from the opening so as not to obstruct the construction of the arch. For a segmental arch, the courses of brick which support the skewback *(below)* should also be built before the arch is constructed.

Arch-builders' jargon. Common terms used to describe the parts of an arch are labelled on the brick arch—a two-ringed segmental arch—on the right, along with the measurements used to plot its shape. The curved inner edge of the arch is called its intrados; the curved edge at the top is the extrados. The under-surface of the arch is the soffit. The masonry or brick walls that support an arch are called abutments. The inclined surfaces of the abutments on which the arch rests are called skewbacks. Each wedge-shaped unit of brick is referred to as a voussoir; a row of voussoirs is called a ring. The centre brick of the lower ring is the key brick.

The imaginary horizontal line between the points where the arch meets the vertical sides of the abutments is called the springing line; the points at which the springing line meets the intrados are the springing points. The rise of an arch is the vertical distance from the springing line to the centre of the intrados. The distance between the abutments is the span of the arch.

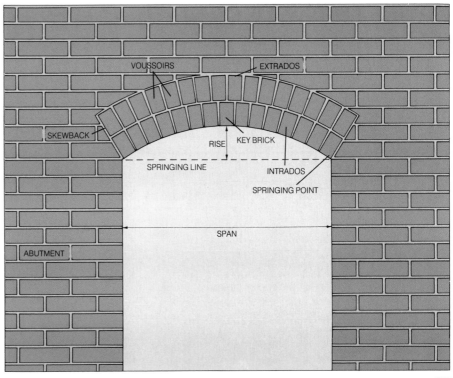

Spanning an Opening with a Half-Circle

Anatomy of a semicircular arch. This example of a semicircular arch is made up of two rings of standard-sized bricks laid on edge in a header pattern. To support such an arch, the abutments must be two bricks thick. For the bricks to follow the curve of the arch, the mortar joints must be made slightly wedge-shaped—thicker at the top than at the bottom, where they should be only 5 mm wide. Because the outside ring follows a wider radius than the inside ring, it requires a greater number of bricks.

The shape of this arch provides great strength because the weight of the bricks in the arch, as well as the weight of the brickwork above it, is carried downwards on to the abutments.

Constructing an Arch with Standard-Sized Bricks

1 **Shaping the centre.** On a sheet of 12 mm plywood, draw a springing line for the arch several centimetres in from the edge. Drive a nail at the centre of the line and use the nail to swing an arc, with wire and a pencil, connecting the ends of the springing line. At the end of the springing line, mark a line at right angles running to the edge of the plywood. Then, with a jigsaw, cut along the line and round the arc.

Using this piece of plywood as a pattern, cut a matching piece. Nail 100 by 50 mm spacer blocks on edge between the two plywood pieces to hold them apart. Position one long spacer with its lower edge along the springing line and shorter pieces around the curved edge, fanning out from the centre like the spokes of a wheel.

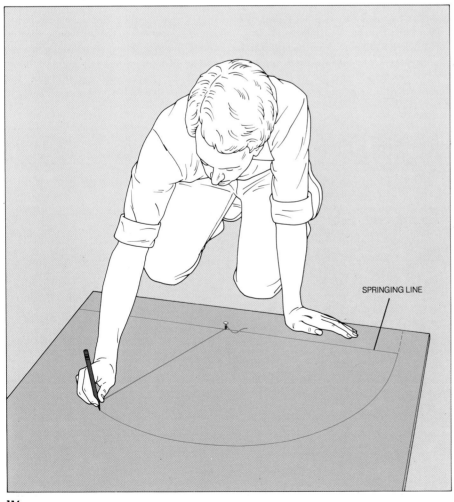

SPRINGING LINE

2 **Marking brick positions.** With the centre laid flat on the ground, assemble an odd number of bricks on end round the curved edge, starting 5 mm above the springing line. Space the bricks 5 mm apart at their inner edges, and position one brick exactly in the centre of the arch; if necessary, increase the gaps between the other bricks to fill out the curve evenly. Mark all the brick positions on the face of the centre.

Arrange a second ring of bricks round the first, leaving a 10 mm gap between rings. Start 5 mm above the springing line, and space the bricks evenly round this second ring. Note the spacing by marking a stick to show the width of a brick plus 5 mm, or whatever is determined by the dry run, for the joint at both ends of the wedge-shaped gaps. Then use this stick as a gauge when you go on to build the outside ring of the arch.

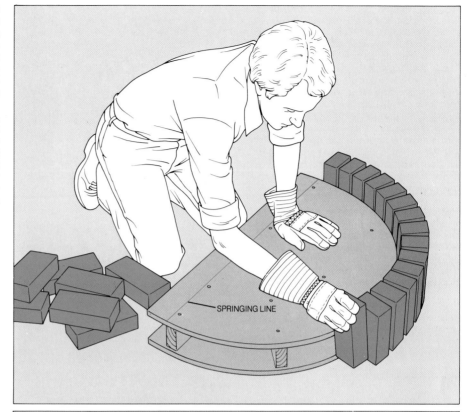

SPRINGING LINE

3 **Setting up the centre.** Nail 100 by 50 mm legs between the plywood faces of the centre, then brace the legs with a 100 by 50 mm crosspiece on each side. To determine the length of the legs, hold the centre in place in the arch opening with the springing line level with the tops of the abutments, while a helper measures the distance between the springing-line spacer block and the ground. Cut the legs to this measurement minus 50 mm. Cut the crosspieces equal in length to the span of the arch.

Raise the centre into the opening, hold a spirit level across the top edges of the two plywood faces and slide folding wedges, cut from 50 by 50 mm timber, beneath the legs *(inset)* to make the centre sit perfectly level. If the centre tends to tip, tighten the wedges, then drive a masonry nail through each leg into mortar joints at the sides of the opening.

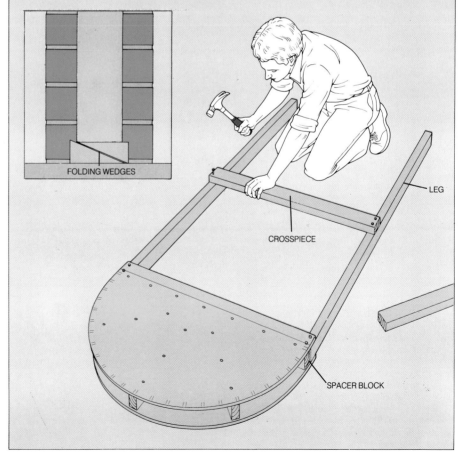

FOLDING WEDGES

LEG

CROSSPIECE

SPACER BLOCK

4 **Beginning the soffit.** Set a bed of mortar for the first brick on top of one abutment, leaving clear 15 mm along the edge that faces the opening; use the blade of the trowel to shape the mortar so that it tapers slightly towards the opening and furrow the joint with the point of the trowel. Lay the first brick on top of the abutment; make sure its soffit face is resting squarely against the centre, and use the handle of the trowel to tamp the brick into the mortar until it fits precisely between the marks on the centre *(right)*. Check with a short spirit level that the brick is level across the width of the wall. Lay a mortar bed on the first brick and position the second brick; continue laying bricks in this manner until you reach about half way up the arch. From here up to the marks made on the centre for the key brick, trowel mortar on to the underside of each brick to be positioned rather than on to the brick already laid, leaving 15 mm clear along the edge facing down into the opening. Build up the other side of the arch in the same way. As you work, raise a mason's line between the corners as a guide to align the front ends of the arch bricks.

5 **Laying the key brick.** Butter one side of the opening awaiting the key brick. Then butter the last brick on one bed side, using the technique shown in Step 4 to shape the mortar so that it tapers slightly towards the soffit face of the brick. Slide the brick into place, tapping it with the trowel handle to wedge it against the centre.

When the mortar has hardened partially, finish all of the joints that will be visible on the completed arch *(page 95)*.

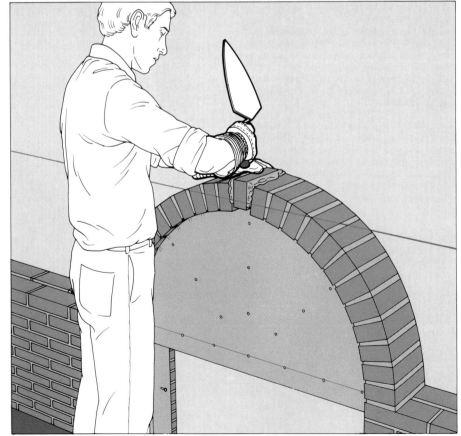

6 **Building the outside ring.** For the second ring lay mortar across the first few bricks of the first ring, then lay a mortar bed on the abutment for the first brick. Start laying bricks from the abutment corners, working towards the centre; when you reach about half way up the first ring of bricks, set mortar on the bed side of each brick to be positioned instead of on the bricks already laid. Tap each brick into the mortar until there is a 10 mm mortar joint between the rings of bricks, checking with the spirit level that each brick is level across the width of the wall.

Pay close attention to the spacing between bricks in the outside ring so that the last bricks will fit when you reach the centre. Use the stick gauge made in Step 2 to shape these joints.

7 **Adding brickwork above the arch.** Fill in horizontal courses of brickwork around the arch, cutting bricks diagonally to meet the curve of the arch. To make a neat diagonal cut, mark the cutting line with a pencil and a ruler on the outer face of the brick; then score the line 12 mm deep using an angle grinder or a circular saw fitted with a masonry blade. Finish the cut by chipping away the waste portion of the brick with the blade end of a bricklayer's hammer. Continue raising courses on both sides until the arch is enclosed.

After the mortar has cured for 24 hours, carefully remove the nails fixing the legs to the wall, and ease the folding wedges by 5 mm. The centre will drop slightly so that the arch takes the weight of the brickwork above it. After the mortar has completely cured, in about five days, remove the wedges while a helper steadies the legs, then ease the centre out from under the arch.

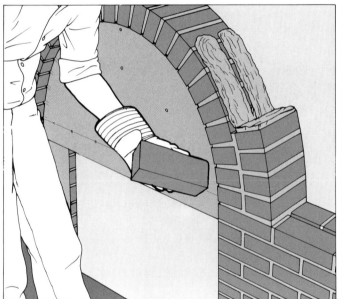

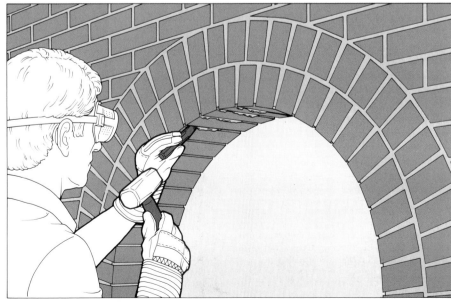

8 **Repointing the soffit.** With a cold chisel and a club hammer, cut out the projecting hardened mortar from the joints of the soffit, clearing them to a depth of 15 mm. Then, using a hawk as a palette, hold a fresh batch of stiff mortar up close to the joints and force new mortar into them with a joint filler. Fill all the joints completely. When the mortar has partially hardened, finish the soffit joints to match those on the face of the arch.

Stone Arches Built to Carry Their Own Weight

The principles and procedures for building a stone arch closely parallel those used for the brick arches shown on the preceding pages. However, the greater complexities of measuring and cutting stone make the work more exacting, and you will probably need a helper to position the heavier stones. You may also require scaffolding on each side of the wall to provide convenient positions for both workers.

Like a brick arch, a stone arch is only as strong as its abutments and foundation footing, to which it transmits outward and downward pressures. The foundation footing between the abutments must be continuous in order to prevent the abutments from slipping, sinking or turning independently of each other. The abutments—whether they are walls (pages 111–114) or freestanding piers—must be left for at least 24 hours for their mortar to set before arch stones are laid between them. The piers for an arch that is not part of a larger wall ought to be at least 300 mm thick, as should the arch itself.

Stones for an arch, like those for a wall, must be strong and weather resistant; but they should also be workable, since you will need to do a lot of precise shaping (pages 106–110). Although single stones that match the thickness of the wall produce the strongest arch, they may be too heavy to handle. Smaller stones can be used in twos or threes to make up the requisite thickness without affecting the strength to any degree. You may even want to use a combination of stones to produce an arch which is slightly thicker than the wall, so that the protruding outer faces will highlight the arch.

For very precise cuts, take your stone and a template of the planned arch to a professional stonemason with facilities for cutting stones of the size you are using. If you make the template from 12 mm plywood, you may be able to use it later as part of the centre which is necessary for building the arch.

The centre for a stone arch is much the same as that used for a brick arch (page 116), but it is thicker because the wall is thicker. The 100 by 50 mm spacers are 25 mm shorter than the wall thickness, and they are positioned with their grain running at right angles to the wall. In the case of a curved arch, the centre is covered with a strip of hardboard to hold the mortar in place until it sets. Because of the great weight of the stones, the centre is supported by four 100 by 100 mm posts, one at each corner. Wooden shims wedge the centre into place and, after the arch has been built, the shims are removed to relieve the compression on the centre assembly. It is then easy to pull out the cross-braced posts and lower the centre.

Use the same semi-dry Portland cement mortar for a stone arch as for a stone wall (page 111). Cut the stones to allow for uniform mortar joints 10 to 15 mm wide and, after the arch is completed, shape the joints to the same depth as the joints in the arch abutments. For maximum safety, allow sufficient time for the mortar to cure completely—it takes roughly 10 days—before you remove the centre assembly.

A Peaked Arch from Two Stone Slabs

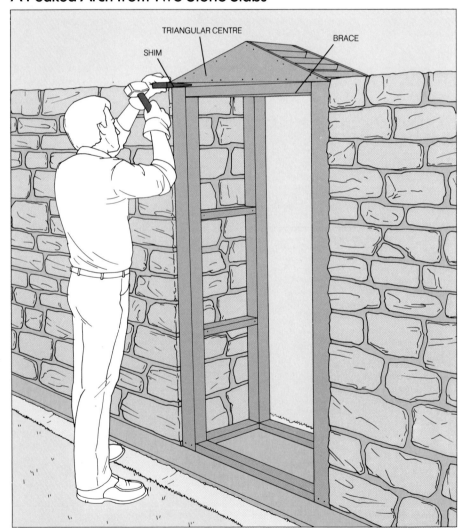

1 Setting up the centre. Make a triangular centre with the desired span and rise as shown on page 116, Step 1, and position it in the opening using wedge-shaped shims to adjust it to the correct height. Support the centre with cross-braced 100 by 100 mm posts cut 12 mm shorter than the height of the springing line. Brace the posts firmly against the abutments with 100 by 50 mm bracing boards at the top and bottom. Insert long wooden shims between the top of each post and the centre. Tap the shims inwards, working alternately on one and then the other, until the centre is raised to the springing line and is levelled.

2 **Setting the skewback stones.** Make a skewback on top of each abutment by selecting or cutting stones to span the thickness of the wall, slanting one end of each stone to form an approximate right angle with the top of the centre. Lay each skewback stone in a 10 to 15 mm bed of mortar, its angled end 12 mm away from the abutment edge. Let the mortar set for 24 hours or more.

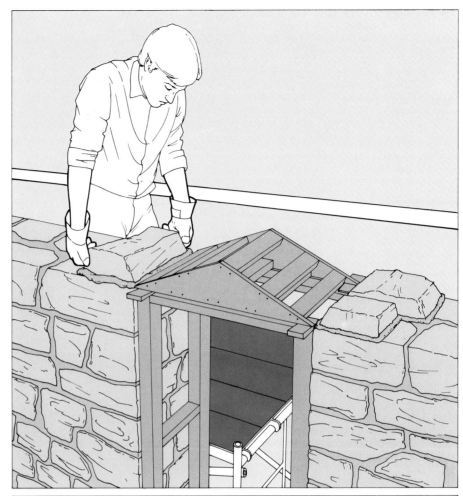

3 **Mitring the lintel stones.** To measure the angled cuts for the peak of the lintel, hold a level at the apex of the centre, perpendicular to the ground, and set the arms of a sliding bevel flush with the centre and the level. To determine the length of each lintel stone, measure the distance from the apex to the bottom of the skewback; deduct 12 mm for a mortar joint at the apex.

Select a paving stone at least 100 mm thick for each lintel; mark the length and the angled cut on the stones. Cut the stones *(page 109),* taking care not to cut them too short. Lay the lintels in place on top of the centre to check their fit. Remove the stones and trim them if necessary.

4 **Laying the lintels.** Throw a 15 mm bed of mortar on the skewback of one abutment, and dampen the first lintel with water. With a helper, lower the stone into place, sliding it down the centre until the end rests in the mortar. Shift the lintel from side to side to position it centrally on the centre, while continuing to press it against the mortar until the joint is 12 mm. For the other lintel stone, throw a 15 mm bed of mortar against the skewback. Butter the apex joint of the second stone with a 15 mm bed of mortar. With your helper, sit the lower edge of the second lintel stone upright on the skewback and lower it carefully on to the centre, compressing the apex joint. Then use a joint filler to compress mortar into the joint at the apex; make sure the apex joint is full and compact to prevent any movement in the arch. Then build the wall in level courses over the arch, bevelling the stones adjacent to the lintel for a close fit *(inset)*.

Allow the mortar to set for at least 48 hours. Then ease the shims slightly so that the centre drops about 5 mm. Remove the centre after 10 days, then repoint and shape the joints on the underside of the lintel as shown on page 114.

A Semicircular Arch
Made from Shaped Stones

1 **Building the centre.** Make a semicircular centre *(page 116)* with a span 12 mm less than the span between the abutments. Cut a strip of 6 mm hardboard as wide as the thickness of the centre and nail it over the arch of the centre, starting at one end and bending the hardboard gently as you fasten it to the edges of the plywood *(right)*. At the opposite end, cut away any excess hardboard.

Lay the centre on its side and drive a nail at the centre of the springing line. Cut a marking string about 500 mm longer than the radius of the arch, and attach the string to the nail.

2 **Pre-fitting the stones.** Select stones for the ends of the arch, preferably single stones as thick as the wall and of similar size. Position them at the ends of the centre with one side flush against the arch. Pull the marking string taut over the bottom edge of one stone and scratch a cutting line with a nail or other sharp implement. Mark the other edge of the stone in the same way. Then mark both edges of the stone at the other end of the centre. Cut the stones along the lines *(page 108)*. You may also need to remove projections from the bottom faces of the stones so that they lie close to the curve of the centre.

Mark lines on the centre corresponding to the cutting lines on the top edges of the first pair of stones. Remove the stones and use the lines on the centre as references for marking the bottom edges of another pair, but leave gaps of 12 to 15 mm between adjacent stones for mortar joints. Continue marking and cutting pairs of stones on opposite sides of the centre, working towards the top. Plan the stones so that they are nearly equal in size, and allow for a single keystone of similar size at the top of the centre. When the layout is complete, number the stones to indicate their positions for assembly.

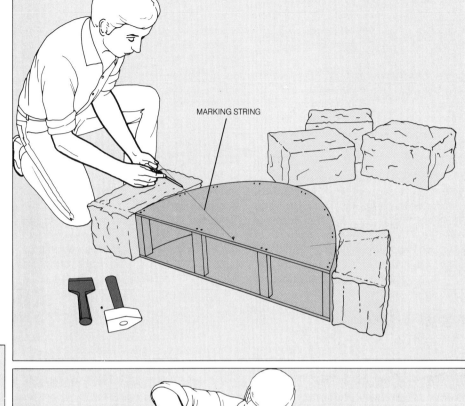

MARKING STRING

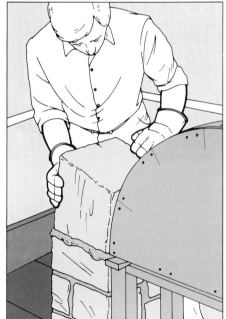

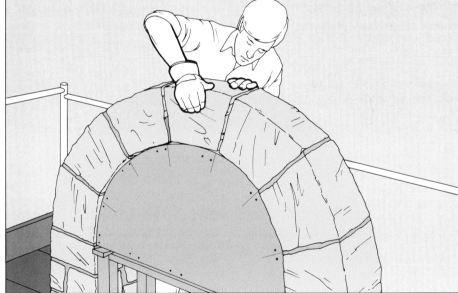

3 **Laying the stones.** Position the centre in the opening *(page 120)*, then lay a 15 mm bed of mortar on one abutment. Dampen the first stone and position it on the mortar bed, centring it on the centre. Twist or rock the stone lightly until it presses the mortar to a 12 mm joint; remove the excess mortar with a trowel.

Set the stone on the opposite abutment in the same manner. Then lay successive pairs of stones until only the gap for the keystone remains.

4 **Setting the keystone.** Add water to mortar until it is the consistency of a very thick paste, then load the mortar on to a trowel and butter the exposed faces of the two stones on either side of the space at the top of the arch. Then gently lower the keystone into the gap, centring it carefully on the centre and between the adjacent stones. As you do so, make sure that you do not push the adjacent stones out of position. Use the same mortar mixture to shape all the accessible joints as shown on page 114.

Let the mortar cure for 72 hours, then ease the shims to lower the centre by about 5 mm. After a further 10 days, remove the centre. Repoint the underside of the arch by cutting a 12 mm recess at each joint with a cold chisel: do not cut the recesses deeper than 12 mm as you could accidentally dislodge one of the arch stones. Then finish the joints to match the pattern of the rest of the arch.

Picture Credits

The sources for the illustrations in this book are shown below. Credits for the illustrations from left to right are separated by semi-colons, from top to bottom by dashes.

Cover: John Elliot. 6: John Elliott. 8–12: Drawings by Oxford Illustrators Ltd. 13: Drawing by Oxford Illustrators Ltd.—drawing by Ray Skibinski. 14–20: Drawings by Oxford Illustrators Ltd. 21: Drawings by Terry Atkinson from Arts and Words. 23: Drawings by Frederic F. Bigio from B-C Graphics. 24, 25: Drawings by Frederic F. Bigio from B-C Graphics, inset renderings, Roger Essley. 26, 29: Drawings by Oxford Illustrators Ltd. 30: Drawings by Gerry Gallagher. 31: Drawing by Gerry Gallagher—drawing by Gerry Gallagher; drawing by Oxford Illustrators Ltd. 33: Drawings by John Massey, except bottom right, by Oxford Illustrators Ltd. 34, 35: Drawings by Oxford Illustrators Ltd. 36: Drawing by John Massey; drawing by Oxford Illustrators Ltd.—drawing by Oxford Illustrators Ltd. 37: Drawing by John Massey—drawing by Oxford Illustrators Ltd. 38, 39: Drawings by Oxford Illustrators Ltd. 40, 41: Drawings by William J. Hennessy. 42: Drawing by William J. Hennessy; drawing by Oxford Illustrators Ltd.—drawing by William J. Hennessy; drawing by Oxford Illustrators Ltd. 43: Drawing by Oxford Illustrators Ltd.—drawings by William J. Hennessy. 44, 45: Drawings by William J. Hennessy. 46, 47: Drawings by Oxford Illustrators Ltd. 48: Drawings by William J. Hennessy—drawing by Oxford Illustrators Ltd. 49: Drawings by William J. Hennessy. 50: John Elliott. 53–57: Drawings by Oxford Illustrators Ltd. 58–61: Drawings by John Massey. 62–65: Drawings by Elsie J. Hennig. 67–81: Drawings by Oxford Illustrators Ltd. 82: Fil Hunter. 85–87: Drawings by Oxford Illustrators Ltd. 88–93: Drawings by Oxford Illustrators Ltd. 94: Drawings by John Massey. 95: Drawings by Oxford Illustrators Ltd. 96–102: Drawings by John Massey. 103: Drawing by John Massey—drawings by Oxford Illustrators Ltd. 104, 105: Drawings by Oxford Illustrators Ltd. 107–110: Drawings by Elsie J. Hennig. 111–114: Drawings by Walter Hilmers Jr., HJ Commercial Art. 115–119: Drawings by Frederic F. Bigio from B-C Graphics. 120–122: Drawings by William J. Hennessy Jr., A and W Graphics. 123: Drawing by Oxford Illustrators Ltd.—drawings by William J. Hennessy Jr., A and W Graphics.

Acknowledgements

The editors wish to thank the following: Brick Development Association, Windsor, Berkshire; Greg Callaghan, Sydney; Cement and Concrete Association, Slough, Berkshire; Michael Curcuruto, Sydney; Tim Fraser, Sydney; Liz Hodgson, London; Graham Patten, London; Vicki Robinson, London; Penny Seabrook, London; Stone Federation, London.

Index/Glossary

Metric Conversion Chart

Approximate equivalents—length

Millimetres to inches		Inches to millimetres	
1	1/32	1/32	1
2	1/16	1/16	2
3	1/8	1/8	3
4	5/32	3/16	5
5	3/16	1/4	6
6	1/4	5/16	8
7	9/32	3/8	10
8	5/16	7/16	11
9	11/32	1/2	13
10 (1cm)	3/8	9/16	14
11	7/16	5/8	16
12	15/32	11/16	17
13	1/2	3/4	19
14	9/16	13/16	21
15	19/32	7/8	22
16	5/8	15/16	24
17	11/16	1	25
18	23/32	2	51
19	3/4	3	76
20	25/32	4	102
25	1	5	127
30	1 3/16	6	152
40	1 9/16	7	178
50	1 31/32	8	203
60	2 3/8	9	229
70	2 3/4	10	254
80	3 5/32	11	279
90	3 9/16	12 (1ft)	305
100	3 15/16	13	330
200	7 7/8	14	356
300	11 13/16	15	381
400	15 3/4	16	406
500	19 11/16	17	432
600	23 5/8	18	457
700	27 9/16	19	483
800	31 1/2	20	508
900	35 7/16	24 (2ft)	610
1000 (1m)	39 3/8	Yards to metres	

Metres to feet/inches		Yards to metres	
		1	0.914
2	6′ 7″	2	1.83
3	9′ 10″	3	2.74
4	13′ 1″	4	3.66
5	16′ 5″	5	4.57
6	19′ 8″	6	5.49
7	23′ 0″	7	6.40
8	26′ 3″	8	7.32
9	29′ 6″	9	8.23
10	32′ 10″	10	9.14
20	65′ 7″	20	18.29
50	164′ 0″	50	45.72
100	328′ 1″	100	91.44

Conversion factors

Length	1 millimetre (mm)	= 0.0394 in
	1 centimetre (cm)/10 mm	= 0.3937 in
	1 metre/100 cm	= 39.37 in/3.281 ft/1.094 yd
	1 kilometre (km)/1000 metres	= 1093.6 yd/0.6214 mile
	1 inch (in)	= 25.4 mm/2.54 cm
	1 foot (ft)/12 in	= 304.8 mm/30.48 cm/0.3048 metre
	1 yard (yd)/3 ft	= 914.4 mm/91.44 cm/0.9144 metre
	1 mile/1760 yd	= 1609.344 metres/1.609 km
Area	1 square centimetre (sq cm)/ 100 square millimetres (sq mm)	= 0.155 sq in
	1 square metre (sq metre)/10,000 sq cm	= 10.764 sq ft/1.196 sq yd
	1 are/100 sq metres	= 119.60 sq yd/0.0247 acre
	1 hectare (ha)/100 ares	= 2.471 acres/0.00386 sq mile
	1 square inch (sq in)	= 645.16 sq mm/6.4516 sq cm
	1 square foot (sq ft)/144 sq in	= 929.03 sq cm
	1 square yard (sq yd)/9 sq ft	= 8361.3 sq cm/0.8361 sq metre
	1 acre/4840 sq yd	= 4046.9 sq metres/0.4047 ha
	1 square mile/640 acres	= 259 ha/2.59 sq km
Volume	1 cubic centimetre (cu cm)/ 1000 cubic millimetres (cu mm)	= 0.0610 cu in
	1 cubic decimetre (cu dm)/1000 cu cm	= 61.024 cu in/0.0353 cu ft
	1 cubic metre/1000 cu dm	= 35.3147 cu ft/1.308 cu yd
	1 cu cm	= 1 millilitre (ml)
	1 cu dm	= 1 litre see **Capacity**
	1 cubic inch (cu in)	= 16.3871 cu cm
	1 cubic foot (cu ft)/1728 cu in	= 28,316.8 cu cm/0·0283 cu metre
	1 cubic yard (cu yd)/27 cu ft	= 0.7646 cu metre
Capacity	1 litre	= 1.7598 pt/0.8799 qt/0.22 gal
	1 pint (pt)	= 0.568 litre
	1 quart (qt)	= 1.137 litres
	1 gallon (gal)	= 4.546 litres
Weight	1 gram (g)	= 0.035 oz
	1 kilogram (kg)/1000 g	= 2.20 lb/35.2 oz
	1 tonne/1000 kg	= 2204.6 lb/0.9842 ton
	1 ounce (oz)	= 28.35 g
	1 pound (lb)	= 0.4536 kg
	1 ton	= 1016 kg
Pressure	1 gram per square metre (g/metre^2)	= 0.0295 oz/sq yd
	1 gram per square centimetre (g/cm^2)	= 0.228 oz/sq in
	1 kilogram per square centimetre (kg/cm^2)	= 14.223 lb/sq in
	1 kilogram per square metre (kg/metre^2)	= 0.205 lb/sq ft
	1 pound per square foot (lb/ft^2)	= 4.882 kg/metre^2
	1 pound per square inch (lb/in^2)	= 703.07 kg/metre^2
	1 ounce per square yard (oz/yd^2)	= 33.91 g/metre^2
	1 ounce per square foot (oz/ft^2)	= 305.15 g/metre^2
Temperature	To convert °F to °C, subtract 32, then divide by 9 and multiply by 5	
	To convert °C to °F, divide by 5 and multiply by 9, then add 32	

Phototypeset by Tradespools Limited, Frome, Somerset
Colour reproduction by Grafascan Limited, Dublin, Ireland
Printed and bound by Artes Gráficas, Toledo, SA, Spain

D. L. TO:1612 -1986